The love and support of Sue Golding, Edward Roy and Richard Vaughan buoys these plays, but they are fondly and passionately dedicated to all the boys (especially Glenn and Shaun and Michael)

"Always in the man, never in the god. But is there a god in this unknown flesh?"
—Pier Paolo Pasolini

CONTENTS

NO TURNING BACK
An Introduction

In the final moments of *More Divine*, the last play in this collection, a young man invites Roland Barthes, its central character, to join him at a new Parisian disco that "used to be a theatre". When Barthes protests that he's too old for such haunts, the boy explains, "It's a place for everybody. You *have* to come. Marcel says it's just *more divine* than anything!" Persuaded by the enthusiasm of his new acquaintance, Barthes embarks for the disco, but only after he enjoins the audience to "Come with us. Come along." His invitation—the last line in the play—cues the descent of massive red drapes and a giant chandelier, a change of scene that initiates the show's climax. To the strains of Poulenc's "Le Repas de Midi", the set opens to frame a large group of people who have been waiting behind the stage. In his directions for the play, Sky Gilbert describes the entrance of these people into the theatre:

> *Fags, dykes, boys, chicks, women, men, whores, old, young — all kinds — appear. Drag queens and marvellously beautiful muscle boys, with grand animal heads, march down a grand staircase. Leather couples gather in the corners and flirt and play. Everyone laughs and begins to dance. The Poulenc ends and disco begins and everyone begins to party.*

For many who attended the premiere production of *More Divine* at Toronto's Buddies in Bad Time Theatre on October 12, 1994, this moment of theatrical transformation was the highlight of the evening. The grand procession of literally dozens of "extras" included artists and technicians who would work at Buddies during the ensuing season, many of them in costume. Perhaps more important, the parade also featured guests from the communities that Buddies primarily serves. Fags, dykes, drag queens and leather couples (many of them in costume …) entered the theatre with the assurance of seasoned performers who know that their time and place has arrived. The audience erupted into sustained applause before moving onto the stage to swell the excited assembly. For many, a sense of history was in the air.

The final coup de théâtre of *More Divine* substantiates the subtitle of the play—"A Performance for Roland Barthes"—by illustrating principles of Barthes' theory of semiology.[1] Specifically, it demonstrates how an event often functions as a sign of social meaning and, further, how signs help to develop cultural myths. Denotatively, the play's final procession signifies Gilbert's repositioning of people traditionally relegated to the margins of Canadian art and society. Spilling over the set and into the centre of the theatre, the parade signals that here, in this time and space, the lives and interests of "marginal" groups are the focus of performance—indeed, they constitute its condition.

The crowd that partied through the opening night of *More Divine* accumulated other, more subtle significations as well—what Barthes terms connotative meaning. Politicians danced with drag queens; actors wearing little more than unicorn masks cavorted with children; a woman in a wheel-chair waved her arms rhythmically to the pounding beat. Together, these actions signify that boundaries traditional to theatrical performance can be crossed and that social barriers, at least temporarily, need not matter. Many in the crowd commented on the "liberating" quality of the event. The sense of occasion strengthened throughout the evening, elevating the party to the mythic proportions that Buddies hoped it would achieve. Through its striking enactment of inclusivity, Buddies swept the crowd into a performance of its future: "overnight", the company moved from the wings of Toronto's theatre community to a position centre-stage.

But the finishing flourish of *More Divine* did more than enact the future of Buddies in Bad Times Theatre; it also embodied the play. Many who entered with the final procession brought a poignant materiality to a speech that Gilbert gives to Michel Foucault near the end of Scene Two. Here, in a fictional meeting with Barthes in 1980, Foucault exclaims that "For every faggot that dies, ten are born, and those ten more are born with a clearer vision of who they are. Why they are here." Perhaps because he is sick with a disease that eventually will be known as AIDS, Foucault's terminology slips at this point from "faggots" to "angels"—to creatures that defy human reason. His slippage is important for it refigures faggots as "unknown flesh"—bodies that defy the categories by which humans organize social groups and, concomitantly, structure relations of power. The fact that a cause and cure for AIDS remain unknown to the institutions of medical practice complicates Foucault's idea. In the play, however, he is less concerned with science's inability to understand the disease than with the consequences of this failure. As he explains to Barthes:

> Many will die. It will be called a plague. Mankind will be called upon to test itself. Mankind will fail the test. In America they will assume that all the undesirables, all the black people, all the sexual people, all the whores will die and the dominant culture will triumph.

Unfortunately, this statement is as relevant today as it was when *More Divine* opened. On that occasion, however, the speech assumed extra significance because of the context in which it was performed. In the moments following his speech, Foucault expounds his vision of faggots reborn as angels: "Look at them!" he cries to Barthes. "Are they turning back? Or are they not just becoming more confirmed more dogmatic more inflexible more passionate more obscene more divine." That the final procession of *More Divine* enacts or, at least, echoes this vision was especially important at the premiere of the show for, on this night, many in the audience were seeing a Buddies production for the first time.[2] And, it is fair to suggest, *everyone* was wondering just what they would see.

People who might never enter a venue devoted to gay, lesbian and alternative theatre attended the premiere of *More Divine* for one main reason. The show inaugurated Buddies' new occupancy of 12 Alexander Street in downtown Toronto, a building owned and financed by public money. For many years the home of Toronto Workshop Productions, a venerated pioneer of Canadian theatre that closed its doors in 1989, the building sits beside a small park near the centre of the city's burgeoning lesbian and gay village. As such, it is the ideal location for Buddies, a company whose mandate unites innovative theatre with queer subjectivities.[3] Despite its carefully designed and presented plans for the site, Buddies fought an up-hill battle to win the City's competition to renovate, manage and program the abandoned facility. Many people, it would seem, worried about the "suitability" of trusting a civic building to an overtly queer theatre.[4] Most of these people had never attended an event at Buddies—a fact they were happy to emphasize to their elected officials and the daily press. Would Sky Gilbert, artistic director of the company, as well as author of *More Divine,* attempt to mollify the conservative sensibilities of the government agencies that finance Buddies' facility by opening the venue with "easy" entertainment? Buddies loyal followers worried about the question as much as the company's opponents feared the answer.

More Divine forestalls any doubts about Gilbert's commitment to his company's mandate. It boldly affirms that, at 12 Alexander Street, there will be no turning back, no matter who pays the bills. Not only will there be more of the alternative programming that has won Buddies solid support within Toronto's fractious theatre community; Buddies new state-of-the-art facility insures that its productions will be "more divine" than ever.

•

Buddies' new home was not only hard-won but a long time coming. The company was formed in 1979 by Sky Gilbert and three other graduates of York University's theatre programme "to explore the relationship of the printed word to theatrical image."[5] Since then, Buddies has redefined its goals by steadily increasing its lesbian and gay content so that now, with its new facility, it claims the status of "the world's largest gay/lesbian/alternative arts centre".[6] The plays in this volume, all originally produced by Buddies, document the resilience of this peripatetic company by tracing its travels from its second rented venue in a warehouse on King Street West in the early 1980s, through two other less than central spaces in downtown Toronto, to its current, permanent home. They also chart the scope and sophistication of Sky Gilbert's work as a playwright during this period, detailing a literary achievement as significant as the theatrical contributions of his company.

DAVID HAWE

D. Garnet Harding, Jason Cadieux, Christopher Sawchyn and Sky Gilbert (left to right)

In the biographical note included in this volume, Gilbert describes himself as a "playwright, poet, actor and drag queen extra-ordinaire". He also lists many of his credits as a filmmaker and a stage director. Perhaps because he is as prolific as he is multi-talented, Gilbert's accomplishments as a playwright remain under-acknowledged, an oversight this collection aims, in part, to redress. Indeed, Jane, the drag persona that Gilbert regularly performs at various public functions, achieves as much notice (or is it notoriety?) as his plays—which speaks more about the voyeuristic fixations of the Canadian media than it does about his talent. It is important to stress that Gilbert *is* all the things he professes, however, for the range and variety of his experience in these capacities informs and invigorates his writing.

The plays in this collection are written by a consummate performer, one for whom *the theatrical* is all. Within his rhetoric of the theatrical (image, gesture, voice, gait), the borders that usually distinguish art from life grow blurry. In this regard, Gilbert's appearances as Jane provide more than photo opportunities: they illustrate how he manipulates performance to both construct and challenge subjectivity on and off the stage. Frequently his plays suggest that the border separating on- and off-stage life is ambiguous, if not arbitrary. For example, the very title of *Theatrelife*, the second play in this collection, implies this idea, as does the structure of the play in which a line of dialogue sometimes cues a scene in *Out to Sea*—an entirely different play that the characters perform in counter-point to the principal drama.

The characters in *Theatrelife* also disrupt the neat separation of audience from performer. Early in the play, Geoffrey Gregson, the artistic director of a large Canadian theatre, is confronted by Lorenzo, an actor in his company, with the protest "I wish you wouldn't turn everything into a play all the time." The line initiates an ironic exchange typical of the self-reflexive moments that Gilbert frequently creates. Gregson replies: "But we are in a play, aren't we? Well, aren't we? Isn't there an audience out there?" While Lorenzo, "*glancing, guilty*" to the audience, answers "No there isn't, of course there isn't," the moment nevertheless invokes a fusion of theatre and life. Geoffrey ends the sequence by overtly emphasizing this fusion: he asks the audience "You don't mind if we just end this scene do you?" A similar incident occurs near the conclusion of the play. Bridget, a female ingenue in Gregson's company who has grown increasingly desperate due to what might be termed "performance confusion", yells at Geoffrey "Does everything have to be a performance?" His answer could be (is ...) Gilbert's: "Oh yes, my dear, yes. Because all the world's a stage and since you're only here once you might as well get a STANDING OVATION!"

The questions, then, are how best to achieve a standing ovation, and for what?—queries particularly pertinent to a performer for whom the audience is a paying entity. In *Theatrelife*, Geoffrey suggests one technique when he admonishes Tom, a male ingenue in his company, to forego the imperatives of "method" acting that lead an actor to search inside himself for the "truth" of a character or scene; he advises the actor to do the opposite, "to lie, to create falsehood, to fabricate reality." Geoffrey cites Laurence Olivier to explain his approach:

> [...] you do know the trick that Olivier had, don't you? It wasn't truth or inner understanding or emotion memory, it was that in

every performance he did something that absolutely amazed the audience, that left them breathless. You must leave them breathless, my boy, and it's much more likely to be a somersault or a handstand or a tumble down three flights of steps than your inner truth.

In his plays, Sky Gilbert frequently leaves me breathless by employing a variety of techniques that work much the way that Geoffrey suggests. In general, Gilbert replaces the conventions of realistic theatre with overt theatricality, disposing "inner truth" for the candid performance of "lies". His approach is not new: indeed, it owes much to the theories of Vsevelod Meyerhold, Bertholt Brecht and Antonin Artaud (the great anti-realists of 20th-century Western theatre) as well as to the traditions of circus, music-hall, cabaret and burlesque. His deployment of the approach, however, investigates new territory—the slippery terrain of queer sex where not only gender roles but also sexual behaviours are mutable, unfixed, open.

It is this uncertain landscape to which the title of this book refers. The unknown flesh of the queer body is as much a theatrical construction as a corporeal entity with material limits. "But is there a god in this unknown flesh?" asks Pier Paolo Pasolini in the epigraph that Gilbert chose for this book. Pasolini's question is loaded with ideological and philosophical freight, for even to ask the question is to presume the possibility that yes, there might be a god inside the man. How, then, should one regard this flesh? Who should name it, govern it, determine its value? These plays do not answer such questions. But they offer what the unknown always provides: the potential for knowing more—and for knowing differently.

•

The primary effect of Sky Gilbert's work for the theatre is the transformation of the audience from isolated consumers of theatrical entertainment to collective participants in oppositional art. He achieves this "trick" by a unique manipulation of strategies associated with postmodern representation: his plays both deconstruct the control of the "real" and reconstruct it as the realm of the possible. Gilbert's singular contribution to Canadian culture is his ability to use high theatricality to fashion culturally transgressive art—and to leave his audience amazed (or aghast) at his audacity.

While Gilbert often relies on poetic or comedic techniques to achieve his theatrical effects, he invariably pursues overtly political agendas. If he is a *bête de la scène*, he also is a pragmatist. Indeed, if such a *bête* exists, he is a queer activist — one for whom the normative order of heterosexuality must be dismantled before it can be reconstructed to accommodate those it presently excludes.[7] Like Barthes, Gilbert recognizes that material conditions form the substance of myths. Ultimately, his "trick" is to "de-doxify"[8] Canadian culture—to make its material conditions seem momentarily "divine."

"Seem" is the operative word here for it summarizes the theatrical style that Gilbert's plays demand. All, in different ways and to varying degrees, expose how theatre makes people (actors) and things (sets) seem to be something else. Like a drag queen who simultaneously conceals and reveals her artifice by wearing nylons with seams, Gilbert reveals the "seams" of his constructions: he exposes, in other words, the methods by which he makes the ordinary seem extraordinary.[9] The technique is clever for it allows him to attempt the reverse as well—to demonstrate how the extraordinary might also be ordinary, how "normal" and "abnormal" are two sides of the same coin, how (to push the metaphor further) the coin is "minted", that is, pressed into existence by social institutions that control its circulation and regulate its worth.

"The only real poetry is to do,/ to act" Pasolini tells a Boy in an early scene of *Pasolini / Pelosi or The God in Unknown Flesh*, the first play in this collection. Pasolini's line summarizes Gilbert's theatrical approach, which is at its most complex in this imagistic play. Pasolini ends Act One by removing a chair from underneath a character, Laura Betti, a trick that leaves her "floating" in mid-air. Pasolini then instructs Laura to sing. She says that she can't. He tells her to "Open your mouth," to open it wide. When she does, "*Out of her comes a lovely singing voice. Music: something religious.*" In this moment of high theatricality, the audience realizes that the actor is not singing—if only because, as in the original production of the play at The Theatre Centre in 1983, her "voice" is accompanied by instrumentation that obviously is recorded. Similarly, the audience understands that the actor does not "actually" float above the floor, even if it cannot discern the harness that holds her adrift. The image, in other words, is a lie. This does not belie its "truth" within the play, however: after the other characters in the scene silently leave the stage, the final Boy "crosses himself" as if in the presence of an apparition. Does the Boy cross himself in reverence or fear, or both? Any answer to this question begs the issues that the play provokes. Is Pasolini a saviour to his Boys, or is he their tormentor? Is he victor or vanquished? Again, is he perhaps both?

The conclusion of *Pasolini / Pelosi or The God in Unknown Flesh* echoes the end of Act One. While Gilbert subtitles the play "A Theatrical Enquiry into the Murder of Filmmaker Pier Paolo Pasolini," it is Pelosi who is murdered on-stage. Gilbert finishes his "enquiry" by having the filmmaker cradle Pelosi in an image evocative of a religious pieta. After Pasolini's other Boys *"steal away"*, he speaks directly to the audience, trying to articulate the nature of his desire for Pelosi—the man who, in real life, was his murderer. His attempts are futile:

> He is what you least expect, he is what you least want to see, he
> is a night last night the night before when you when you … when
> you … he is when you he is when you ….

Finally, in his frustration, Pasolini resorts to an extended scream, the inscrutable cry that ends the play. Although the sequence is difficult to interpret, the play's title—or, more accurately, the *slash* in the title—provides a clue for it links both men in a single sign. It allows, in other words, that Pasolini and Pelosi are two halves of the same coin. Because they complete each other, they suffer the same pain, no matter which of them dies.

Pasolini's inability to describe the feelings that lead him to pursue his murderer in *Pasolini / Pelosi* presumes that his desire is unknown to most people in the audience. He begins his last speech by explaining:

> I am drawn to him the him that very few of you see that I have
> seen that he shows to me on dark steamy nights and the street-

corners and the so what that he shows himself in different guises,
in different ways so what he plays a game so what?

Gilbert constructs Pasolini's unknown desire by transgressing
the rules and conventions of "correct" syntax, foregoing punctua-
tion, for example, before he resorts to complete elision and, finally,
noise (the scream). When Gilbert returns to the figure of Pasolini in
the third play in this collection, he again constructs the filmmaker's
desire as an obsession that is unknown to the majority of the audience. This time, however, he is more overt about Pasolini's fascina-
tions and, as a result, more direct about the moral questions they
incite.

The situation of *In Which Pier Paolo Pasolini Sees His Own
Death in the Face of a Boy* is similar to *Pasolini / Pelosi* in that Gilbert
once again has Pasolini seduce the young Boy who subsequently
murders him. And, as in his earlier play, Gilbert presents the narra-
tive in a highly theatrical manner. This time, however, Gilbert
replaces physical and verbal poetry with theatrics that are more confrontational in style and effect. In his notes on the setting of the production at Buddies' last rented venue at 142 George Street where
the show premiered in 1991, Gilbert explains that "Many of the
monologues and some of the scenes were performed in the audience." In fact, a number of the scenes require the actors to address
members of the audience one-on-one, which they did with tense
concentration during the premiere. The opening stage directions,
for example, state that the actor playing Pasolini enters the theatre
and "*walks intently over to an audience member and pulls up a chair
and sits opposite him or her.*" Gilbert also explains in his note that
"Certain scenes were played beside the audience near the exit doors
of the theatre so that the audience could not hear or see everything."
Indeed, one of the crucial scenes in the play is performed entirely in
the dark.

The vacillation in the staging of this play between "in your face"
delivery and deliberate obscurity parallels the dialectic that Pasolini
introduces with his opening speech to the unsuspecting audience
member: "Should I? Moral question. I have met a questionable boy.
A boy of questionable. Hah. Origin. Hah. Morals. Hah. He is questionable. What do you think? Do you think I should go with him?"

This interrogative technique is compounded by sequences where both Pasolini and the Boy speak simultaneously to individual audience members about their assignation. After a blackout mid-play, the two actors reappear at a table eating chocolate cake, "*stylish kerchiefs around their necks*". Their subsequent conversation indicates that they have assumed new characters, Goodness and Gracious, who debate the moral issues introduced by Pasolini during his encounter with the Boy in the first half of the play. Near the end of that encounter, Pasolini rails against the constraints that condemn a range of activities including the "crimes" he desires to commit:

> There is an order must be an order no incest no rape no murder no deceit no stealing no homosexuality no coveting lusting wanting spewing stalking obsession desire beyond the point where it, sensibly, produces children. What would happen if these rules were to be broken?

In the second half of the play, Gracious, who is performed by the same actor who plays Pasolini, asks a variation of the question: "What should be done with those people who violate basic moral laws?"

This short play doesn't answer the question; rather, it confounds it by positing others. Like Pasolini who induces the Boy to participate in acts that many find repugnant if not criminal, Gracious poses questions that eventually lead Goodness to murder him in a fit of disgust. In both scenarios, moral outrage at illicit desire incites murder. This situation forces the audience to consider not only its (in)tolerance of obscure acts of "unknown" flesh but, also, to interrogate the moral imperatives that justify the murder of people who transgress.

In the last line before the blackout that precedes the appearance of Goodness and Gracious, Pasolini states: "I want to undo all that has been done and go back to a very frightening place where there are no answers and, I fear, no microwave ovens." In this play (arguably the most provocative in this collection), Gilbert takes the audience to just such a place, providing an ironic fillip before he leaves it to consider the unfamiliar terrain. In the final moments of *In Which Pier Paolo Pasolini* ..., the actors drop their roles to address themselves by their real names; at this point, they also apologize to the audience for the "nasty subjects" and "disgusting situations" presented in the play. In a "sweet" display of liberal sentiment, they explain that "what we've discovered is most important about life is just plain old-fashioned warmth and affection. Not sex. Just love." As they "*smile out at the audience*," there is "*a burst of applause on tape.*" In the following blackout, the final lines of the play render their comments sarcastic. Pasolini says: "You want it ... I know you want it ... I always know when you guys want it ...." Lights flash quickly to reveal that "*Pasolini is terrified. He stares at the Boy.*" After the final, brief blackout, the lights come up on the audience, alone.

•

In his plays Gilbert uses ambiguity to question the separation of art from life as well as to interrogate moral and cultural values. One of the values to which he consistently returns is love. Not surprisingly, his depictions of love vary from the usual. Besides focussing on same-sex couples, love in Gilbert's plays often eschews the conventions of heterosexual romance to embrace a diversity of forms that might otherwise pass unnoticed. Once again, Gilbert works in opposition to dominant ideologies of feeling and affect, substituting imaginative responses for bankrupt emotions.

My Night With Tennessee deals with a much-told tale— Tennessee Williams' attraction to adolescent boys, a "compulsion" reputed to have contributed to his despair and demise. As in the other plays in this volume, Gilbert recasts Williams' desire to fashion an alternative to the melodramatic treatment it frequently receives.[10] Once again, his method utilizes a performance inside the play. This time, Jamie Angell, a fifteen-year-old boy that Williams meets in a restaurant, recites "The Hill", a poem by Rubert Brooke, after he consents to strip to his underwear during a visit to Williams' hotel room in Vancouver. Before Jamie begins his recitation, Tennessee "*adjusts a light on Jamie so it is perfect*", literally highlighting the theatricality of the boy's performance. The moment is reminiscent of those where Pasolini rehearses Laura Betti and his Boys, and where Geoffrey Gregson directs his actors. In this case, however, Jamie Angell is not an actor (though, of course, he is); after

Jamie reads Brooke's poem, Williams calls him "a gracious and charming young man" before he instructs him to "put your clothes back on".

Jamie's performance for Tennessee, while not as overt as a play-within-a-play, has the same result: it foregrounds the theatricality of the play and thus displaces its realistic effect. This is particularly important in *My Night with Tennessee* where *reactions* to performance are as much the focus as performance itself. After listening to the boy's recitation, Tennessee cries. Ineffectively, he rationalizes to Jamie that "that poem always makes me cry ... because Rupert Brooke is such a damned awful poet ...." But the boy, in his concern for Williams' feelings, argues "I don't see why you say he's such a bad poet. I liked the poem." Tennessee's subsequent speech offers insight into a criticism that his own plays, as well as Gilbert's, sometimes illicit:

> Well I like it too, but it is, if I may, so — so unreservedly sentimental, and art should not be that way, if it can possibly be avoided. But sometimes it is, and we cry about silly things we can't change.

Later, after Jamie has left, Williams lies in bed with Crummy Mullins, his partner in the play. Tennessee explains that Jamie's recitation reminded him of Frank, whose name he inadvertantly used to bid the boy goodbye. For those in the audience who know that Williams had a long-time companion named Frank Merlo, the moment gains added poignancy.[11] Gilbert immediately disrupts the sentimentality that this moment might cause, however, by having Williams explain to Crummy that "Frank wasn't even Frank." He elaborates:

> Frank is an idea. An idea of something that can never be gotten a hold of. So when you find that [*he sniffles*] I'm looking for Frank, or thinking about him or searching the eyes of boys for Frank, just remember nobody is Frank, and not even Frank was Frank.

The attitude to sentimentality that Gilbert offers in his construction of Williams is contradictory, which befits a play that dramatizes a paradox. In *My Night with Tennessee*, Williams wants to relive an experience of deferral, of a desire that was only pursued, never fulfilled. Williams realizes that Frank, the focus of his lve, was ultimately unknowable, a person whose "true" nature he only could imagine. In *Hester: An Introduction*, Gilbert illustrates this idea again, substituting comic frustration for the melancholy of the earlier work.

Gilbert structures *Hester* with a rapid series of short scenes in which a drag queen, "*beautiful, tragic and funny*", repeatedly responds to a knock on her door by opening it to different results. The play enacts the process of deferral that Williams describes in the earlier play. Here, however, Gilbert makes the audience, not Hester, wait to see the "introduction". When, eventually, "*A Man in a trench coat enters* [...] *wearing sunglasses and a fedora*," all that Hester can do is stare, "*confused*". The Man walks downstage to a microphone which he uses to introduce himself to the audience. Rather than explain who he is, the Man states: "I will be everything you want except a couple of things which are very important to you. Those things will be missing." As his voice mutates through various registers provided by the manipulation of the sound equipment, he grows increasingly "*embarrassed*" in his monologue. The play ends with Hester still upstage listening "*sadly, bemused* [...] *humiliated*" as the Man says "I'm not very ... very good at this ... sorry ...."

Like the search for love, the will to know another person leads many of the characters in these plays to undertake a variety of risks. Some, like Hester, suffer disappointment; others are misunderstood, reviled or, as in the case of Pasolini, destroyed. Nevertheless, they pursue their hazardous goals for as long as they can. Like Tom in *Theatrelife*, they repeatedly assert that their lives gain greater meaning when they are lived dangerously—when consciousness of mortality, for example, makes each moment more precious. Perhaps this is why, in *Theatrelife*, Gilbert figures love like AIDS— as a disease that lacks either a verifiable cause or a potential cure. In this play, Tom assures Geoffrey that he will love regardless of the consequences. Speaking of love, he says "This disease, it repels; but in a strange way, it attracts. It bewitches, it alarms, it keeps us in suspense."

For many of Gilbert's characters, the search for love involves libidinous pursuits that society still condemns. For some of his audience, this presents a challenge inasmuch as these pursuits appear as strange in life as they seem in the theatre. For many others, however, his plays affirm an experience of the world in which difference inspires resistence as much as it incites rejection. Collectively, these plays do more than investigate the boundaries between life and art: they also explore the ineffable. Like blood in unknown flesh, desire courses through them with vital urgency—unnameable and defiant.

ROBERT WALLACE
TORONTO, SEPTEMBER 1995

NOTES

1. See Roland Barthes, "Myth Today", *Mythologies*, trans. Annette Lavers (London, 1972), 117-174.
2. Sky Gilbert's direction of the premiere production of *More Divine* made the connection between Foucault's speech and the final procession more explicit by staging the ascent of an actor costumed as an angel from a trap in the floor of the stage during the final moments of the parade.
3. In the brochure advertising its 1995-96 season, Buddies includes the following as part of its mission statement:

    Buddies in Bad Times Theatre is an artist-run, non profit, queer theatre company committed to the development and production of radical new Canadian work. As a pro-sexual company, we celebrate difference, and challenge the professional theatre experience by blurring and reinventing boundaries between: artistic disciplines, performer and audience, gay and lesbian, queer and straight, male and female, good and bad [....]

    For a full discussion of the evolution of Buddies in Bad Times Theatre from its inception to the present, see my article "Theorizing a Queer Theatre: Buddies in Bad Times" in *Contemporary Issues in Canadian Drama* ed. Per Brask (Winnipeg, 1995), 136-159.
4. For a summary of the selection process by which Buddies was picked to run the 12 Alexander Street facility, see the final chapters of Neil Carson's book *Harlequin in Hogtown: George Luscombe and Toronto Workshop Productions* (Toronto, 1995).

5. Sky Gilbert, quoted by Patricia Keeney-Smith in "Living With Risk: Toronto's New Alternate Theatre", *Canadian Theatre Review* 38 (Fall 1983), 35.

6. See Buddies' 1995 advertising materials for the use of this term—for example, the back cover of the programme for its annual 4-Play festival (2-14 May 1995).

7. In his Introduction to *Fear of a Queer Planet: Queer Politics and Social Theory* (Minneapolis, 1993), editor Michael Warner discusses "a heteronormative understanding of society" that queer subjects work to subvert.

8. In *The Politics of Postmodernism* (London and New York, 1989), Linda Hutcheon adapts Barthes notion of *doxa* "as public opinion or the 'Voice of Nature' and consensus" to propose that postmodern representations work to "de-toxify" the political import of cultural forms. See page 3 *passim*.

9. Drag figures prominently in Sky Gilbert's plays. Indeed, two of his best known plays—*Drag Queens on Trial* and *Drag Queens in Outer Space*—utilize males who impersonate females. Others such as *Lola Starr Builds Her Dream Home* and *Suzie Goo: Private Secretary* have provided Buddies with some of its biggest hits. Of the plays in this volume, only *More Divine* and *Hester: An Introduction* feature an extended use of the technique. For useful discussions of drag and its relationship to "camp" see *Camp Grounds: Style and Homosexuality*, ed. David Bergman (Amherst, 1993).

10. See, for example, Dotson Rader, *Tennessee: Cry of the Heart* (Garden City, 1985).

11. See *Tennessee Williams' Letters to Donald Windham 1940-1965*, ed. Donald Windham (New York, 1977).

PASOLINI / PELOSI, OR THE GOD IN UNKNOWN FLESH: A THEATRICAL INQUIRY INTO THE MURDER OF FILMMAKER PIER PAOLO PASOLINI

Pasolini / Pelosi, or The God in Unknown Flesh: A Theatrical Enquiry into the Murder of Filmmaker Pier Paolo Pasolini was first produced by Buddies in Bad Times Theatre at The Theatre Centre, 666 King Street West, Toronto, in April 1983, with the following cast:

PASOLINI Damir Andrei
BOY 1 Angelo Pedari
BOY 2 Daniel Allman
BOY 3 Frank Pellegrino
LAURA BETTI Arlene Mazerolle

Director: Sky Gilbert
Assistant Director: Ken McDougall
Set and Lighting Designer: Patsy Lang

Characters

PASOLINI, mid-thirties, the Italian twentieth-century poet, film-maker and gay activist

BOY 1 (also plays PELOSI, the teenaged boy convicted of murdering Pasolini; LION; NURSE)

BOY 2 (also plays BOY with LION)

BOY 3 (also plays DEVIL/ANGEL, a bourgeois Italian actor; DOCTOR; BOURGEOIS HOMO)

LAURA BETTI, mid-thirties, the actress and friend of Pasolini (also plays GIRL with LION; RITA HAYWORTH; BOURGEOIS LADY; RADIO REPORTER; PEASANT WOMAN; PROFESSOR)

Time

1975.
Various.

Setting

In the original production, the staging was simple and relied mainly on lighting. Large swaths of fabric were used to create a scrim, to define acting areas and to create the effect of a long alley. In Prologue One an 8mm-film projector was used to project the image of an actual lion onto the actor. This same projector was used in Act One to flash light on another actor to create the illusion of a flickering film image. LAURA BETTI convincingly "flew" with the aid of a hidden harness (hooked to a cord behind a post).

PROLOGUE ONE

Lights up. A little BOY *and* GIRL *appear, dressed in Arabian costumes*

BOY Come with me.
GIRL But where are we?
BOY Come with me.

[*A* LION *appears. The little* BOY *stares at him. The little* GIRL *cringes in fear*]

GIRL Oh no! We will be killed!
BOY No, we will not. This lion does not roar.

[*The* LION *opens its mouth*]

You see? I am the lion's son, transformed into a prince.

[*The little* BOY *lies down in the* LION's *arms*]

The lion loves me. He will love you too.
GIRL But I am afraid!
BOY But you must let the lion love you, you must make the lion smile.

[*The* LION's *face turns into the face of* PELOSI, PASOLINI's *killer.* PELOSI *is smiling sweetly*]

GIRL But he will kill you.
BOY [*leaning back*] He only kills those who are afraid. See? [*he relaxes*] You must make the lion smile.

[*Music: something Arabic. The little* GIRL *rests in the* LION*'s arms with the little* BOY *as lights fade to black*]

PROLOGUE TWO

The stage is dimly lit
A street boy, PELOSI, *sits partially hidden behind a scrim.* PELOSI *is*
trying to learn his lines for a movie in which he plays PASOLINI*'s ideal*
beauty. Dimly viewed to the sides of the scrim are the DEVIL/ANGEL
and PASOLINI
PELOSI *says his lines slowly and carefully. He begins when* PASOLINI
nods

PELOSI You will not recognize me when you meet me. Each time, you
suspect, will be the last. You expect me, I do not seem to expect
you at all. I frighten you. I make you smile. Of this you are certain. That I will make you feel uncertain. I will make you feel that
you are on shaky ground. I will upset you. I will make you cry. I
will make you wonder and suspect. Not many others will like me
or maybe they will. My entrance will be unexpected my exit
painful my smile compelling. Of this you are certain: I will make
you feel uncertain. Of this you are certain. That I will make you
feel uncertain. And this uncertainty is something that you ache
for, that you long for. You long not to know. You long to be
afraid. You long for once to be uncertain, to be afraid. Not to
know. [*he looks up at* PASOLINI *for approval*] Bene?
PASOLINI Bene.

ACT ONE

The stage gradually lightens. Music: "Winter" from The Four
Seasons, Vivaldi. *It is a filming day.* BOYS *are all about, fixing
things, hanging from light stands.* PASOLINI *walks in, hands his coat
to a* BOY *and begins talking about his memories of Casarsa*

PASOLINI The houses of old Casarsa are arranged in such a way—for
they are old, very old, stony, brackish, livestock behind crumbling
walls—that occasionally one imagines in them the influence of the
Renaissance. A painting perhaps in darkish colours. It's a summer
evening. I am riding my bicycle. I have passed through this village
and that. Ahhh, San Giovanni, someone singing or is it just some
ungodly murmur, a throbbing echo? It's wet. The endless lamps
are flickering. Peasants whisper something half heard on some for-
gotten summer that makes me remember ... Boys call to each other
across a gigantic square. They're playing a game. A sudden, unexpected shout. It's twilight, or at least almost night. And then ...

[*The* BOYS *run off, except for* BOY 2, *a sixteen-year-old, who remains,
kicking a can.* PASOLINI *watches him for a moment*]

Hello.
BOY 2 Hi. [*he kicks the can aimlessly*]
PASOLINI What are you doing there? [*he kneels down*]
BOY 2 Nothing.

[*He moves around, looks at* PASOLINI, *and then looks back down.
Pause*]

I wish ...

PASOLINI What do you wish ...
BOY 2 [*looking at him*] I wish ...
PASOLINI [*imitating him*] I wish ...
BOY 2 [*looking at him, then looking down*] I wish I had ...
PASOLINI I wish I had ...
BOY 2 [*suddenly challenging*] Hey— What are you doing?
PASOLINI [*smiles, this is what he likes*] Nothing.

[*Pause*]

Go on ... I wish I had ...
BOY 2 [*looking at him mischievously*] A ... soccer ball.
PASOLINI A soccer ball.
BOY 2 Yeah.
PASOLINI I see.
BOY 2 I don't have one.
PASOLINI Don't the other boys have one?
BOY 2 No. Nobody does. [*he is mischievous again*] I want one.
PASOLINI Well.

[*Pause*]

You could get one.

[*Pause*]

BOY 2 How?
PASOLINI I could get you one.
BOY 2 Go on. [*he laughs*]
PASOLINI I'm serious.

[*Pause*]

You want me to get it for you?

[*Pause*]

BOY 2 What do I ... gotta do?

PASOLINI What?
BOY 2 You know. What's the catch?
PASOLINI No catch.
BOY 2 No catch?
PASOLINI No.

[*Pause*]

You meet me here at about eight and I'll give you the ball ...
okay?
BOY 2 [*smiling*] Okay.

[PASOLINI *laughs and ruffles* BOY 2*'s hair*]

PASOLINI Okay.
BOY 2 Hey, you watch out, eh?
PASOLINI [*getting up*] Sure.
BOY 2 [*laughing*] I gotta watch out for you—
PASOLINI Yeah, you do.
BOY 2 I do.

[*They stare at each other*]

See ya.

[*He turns and runs away a bit, then stops*]

Hey.
PASOLINI Yeah?
BOY 2 You look like Jack Palance.
PASOLINI I do?
BOY 2 Yeah.

[*Pause*]

I gotta watch out for you. [*he laughs*] I gotta watch out for you.

[*He runs off. Pause*]

PASOLINI Jack Palance.

[*Pause. He feels his face*]

I guess I do. Interesting.

[*He sits down and plays with the can, quietly*]

Now, you see, he will go back home to his father who is drunk
and out of work. His father beats him and calls him a monster.
He's jealous of his son's growing prick. Me, I'm not jealous. I love
the little monster. I just want to give the kid a soccer ball and if he
wants ... [*looking off*] and I think he does want, I'll make him
come. [*pause*] When his father dies, they'll erect a monument and
sing "himmmmms". When I die—if some jealous father doesn't
shoot me first—they'll call me pederast. Except for the boys.
They'll call me Jack Palance. In fact, I do look a little like him.
[*he feels his face again*] I do.

[*He starts to wander off*]

I do.

> [*The music of pots and pans clanking is heard.* BOY 1, BOY 2
> BOY 3 *and* LAURA BETTI *enter. The* BOYS *perform a playlet
> about a boy and a pig.* LAURA *narrates.* PASOLINI *sits in his
> director's chair and reads the lines for the imaginary pig and
> Spinoza*]

> BOYS "The Boy Who Loved a Pig".
> [*singing*] *There once was a boy*
> *Once was a boy*
> *A boy who loved a pig*
> *His dreams were very small*
> *But his heart was very big*
> *Late at night*
> *Late at night*
> *He crept into the sty*

And momma and poppa they always asked
Why oh son oh why
Why oh son oh why
He loved a pig
Why oh son oh why?

BOY 3 *I am the father look at me*
I like to drink but more than tea.

BOY 1 *I am the mother oh watch me cry*
I hate to see my son go in a sty.

BOY 2 *I am the son, who is not very happy*
I love my momma and hate my pappy.

PASOLINI I am the pig. I have no opinions.

LAURA [*narrating*] Luncheon at home.

BOY 3 Eat faster you little pig!

BOY 2 Sorry.

BOY 1 Don't shout at him. He is a lovely boy. Don't you like his fuzzy ears?

[*The three* BOYS *guzzle their invisible food for a moment*]

Listen to him snort, the little sow.

[BOY 1 *ruffles* BOY 2*'s hair*]

Isn't our son a darling?

BOY 3 Hah. [*he takes a swig of liquor*] You'll drive me to drink with your grunts.

[BOY 3 *pulls* BOY 2*'s head*]

Get your head out of that trough.

BOY 2 Sorry.

BOY 1 Don't be hard on him darling honey-bunches. My little piglet.

[BOY 1 *kisses* BOY 2]

My hoggywoggy.

[As the lights dim, a spotlight shines on LAURA*]*

LAURA *[narrating]* It was clear where the problem began. It
was all his mother's fault. For loving the pig in him. And
his father's fault too, for shouting anti-pig sentiments at
the breakfast table. No wonder the sensitive young son
turned to the sty for his perverted consolation!

*[*BOY 2 *is wandering in the darkness]*

BOY 2 Every exquisite moment of my adolescence
was filled with the touching sweetness of love.
I imagine him still
reading among the flowers
flowers with no memory of passion.
Jesus loves me this I know
for the Bible drowns in his blood.

[Lights up on the imaginary pig. BOY 2 *sees the pig]*

O pig, pig. There is something
simple and unpretentious in your
curly tail and hairy hide. I must have
you: I must have you now. Here, in this
sty in the moonlight. You don't mind, do you?

[He lies down with the pig and starts to make love]

My love is greater than the ocean,
higher than the sea.
Put on your pig wings
and fly with me ...

[Lights dim on BOY 2. *Lights up on* BOY 3]*

LAURA *[narrating]* Father at a board meeting.
BOY 3 Profits fall
And we wonder why

Not enough work
Not enough greed
Not enough cruelty
Not enough selfishness and ambition.
Also our penises are much smaller than the competing
companies! We must hire men with larger penises!

BOY 1 [*as a secretary*] Excuse me sir.

BOY 3 Yes, what is it honey? I'm in a meeting.

BOY 1 Well sir,
Your son has been found in a sty
no one seems to know why but
he seems to love a pig.

BOY 3 [*upset*] That is a big
problem.
Go away honey
make some coffee.

LAURA [*narrating*] But the story was out
That was the end of the
father's career.
When they heard that his
son was in love with a pig
They all quit the company
and the father was without
profits.

BOY 3 Without profits I am nothing.
Come back my fellow employees!
I denounce my son.
I am normal.
I don't love pigs at all!

LAURA [*narrating*] But it was no use. And the son wailed
ashamed, unsure with his pig, who gave him
no reassurance.

BOY 2 O blessed be the sinner, me
I am more sinned against
My glorious indiscretions when revealed
are almost beautiful and resemble
a certain trick of theatrical lighting
Jesus loves me and trains a spotlight

on all my wrongs which are too many to
enumerate here!

LAURA [*narrating*] And then one night, in the sty when
the boy was lying with his one and
only, the giant pig, Spinoza appeared
to him and justified his actions.

[*Light blazes and choral music begins to play*]

PASOLINI [*as Spinoza*] It's alright to love a pig
Because God is in all things
A tree is not holier than a pig
And neither is a woman
Drink from the fruit of life and love
And don't listen to the teachings
of the Old Testament, too much.

BOY 2 O I am vindicated I am justified
I love you pig and I am proud of it
O I'll yell my secret to the whole world
My eyes will again belong to me
and my loneliness will have the power of music!

[*The* BOYS *begin dancing and singing*]

BOYS *There once was a boy*
Once was a boy
A boy who loved a pig
His dreams were small
His dreams were small
But his heart was very big
Late at night
Late at night
He crept into the sty
And Momma and Poppa they always asked
Why oh son oh why
he loved a pig
Why oh son oh why.

[BOYS 2 & 3 *dance off, leaving* BOY 1 *alone on the stage*]

BOY 1 [*sadly*] Such a nice ... boy
The wedding will be muddy!
I wish that pig could play the piano ...

[BOY 1 *hums and smiles maternally, then runs off with a
boyish "whoop!" The little playlet is over*]

[*Lights up on* PASOLINI *who sits smoking, staring at* LAURA. *Through
sunglasses, she stares back at him; she too smokes. He is directing her
in a crucial scene, manipulating her psychologically in order to get
what he wants*]

PASOLINI Laura talk.

[*Pause*]

Laura talk. [*to the crew and other cast*] She doesn't talk.
LAURA [*adamant*] I *don't* talk.

[*Pause*]

She is not inclined to talk.

[PASOLINI *goes up to* LAURA *with intense excitement*]

PASOLINI But you know I like her. I *really* like her. [*he thinks, stares at
her and turns away*] Laura disagree! Laura disagree!
LAURA I don't talk. [*she's frustrated with the part*] I have nothing to say.

[PASOLINI *suddenly picks her up. She beats him with her fists*]

Animale! You are an *animale!*

[PASOLINI *puts her down, slowly*]

PASOLINI An inscrutable woman.

LAURA [*staring into his eyes, confused*] What, hey? What hey? [*she becomes sexually grounded. She sways her hips and gets into the part*] What, hey …

PASOLINI And sometimes, out of her mind. [*he begins the speech for her*] That's not true, I'm as sane as the rest of you, he says, his hands on his stomach, his mouth—

LAURA [*trying the text one final time*] That's not true, I'm as sane as the rest of you, he says, his hands on his stomach, his mouth on his cigar, his feet marching, that's not true. [*she is excited and confuses the words*] I'm as sane as the rest of you he says his hands on his mouth his feet on his cigar, his stomach—

PASOLINI Enough, Laura. Enough.

LAURA [*sitting down*] Enough?

PASOLINI Enough. [*he calmly coaxes her along*] But best of all, she can be silent. She knows how to be silent.

LAURA [*serene*] Yes.

PASOLINI Yes?

LAURA Yes.

PASOLINI She knows how to say … yes.

LAURA [*serene, like the Madonna*] Yes …

[LAURA *smiles and an image of the Madonna appears over her head. Music: something religious. Lights dim. Lights up again on another film set. It is outdoors.* PASOLINI *is filming a scene about a boy and a bicycle*]

PASOLINI Come on, let's get going. Hurry up, over here.

BOYS Alright, okay.

PASOLINI [*making a signal to start*] Camera—

[*The performance begins.* BOY 2 *is on a bike*]

BOY 1 What's he—

BOY 3 That's my line Paolo— He stole my line—

BOY 1 No. My line is "What's he doing?" Yours is "I don't know."

[*The two* BOYS *fight amongst themselves*]

PASOLINI Wait, wait, let's start again— Go.

> BOY 1 What's he doing?
> BOY 3 I don't know.

PASOLINI [*whispering to* BOY 2] Where are you going?

> BOY 2 [*proudly*] To the sky!

> [*He begins to ride away*]

PASOLINI [*narrating*] His hair covering his face, the boy leans over to fix his bicycle. His blue uniform is like a silken cord between earth and heaven.

> [BOY 2 *reaches an area of blue light, behind the scrim*]

There's the sky. He looks up. The paths wind through the hills and flying perilously high atop is a steeple. He has reached ...

> [BOY 2 *stops his bike*]

His blue sky!
> BOY 2 Buon giorno, Paolo!

> [*He waves and rides off*]

> BOY 1 What's he doing?
> BOY 3 I don't know.

BOY 1 [*shouting at* PASOLINI] This is stupid, it's crazy— What is this shit? It's stupid, stupid, stupid. It doesn't make any sense—
PASOLINI There's nothing to make sense. It's a movie about peasants. That's why I chose you.
BOY 1 Oh yeah, you big Communist with lots of money. Communists always have money, if you're so goddamned concerned about the peasants why don't you go out there and fucking do something

about it, eh?

PASOLINI Culture in Italy is still bourgeois.

BOY 1 And you're still bourgeois— What have you ever done for politics, just this stupid movie about poor peasants— You're a fake. You're just a fucking intellectual. That's what's wrong with you, you don't know anything about poor people. I'm poor—I know—

PASOLINI But now you have a salary—

BOY 1 Yeah big man, I don't have a big salary like yours—

PASOLINI Listen to me—

Okay, so I'm a poet.

Screw that.

[BOY 1 *moves away in disgust*]

No, listen.
I wish I could just do it, you know, be in it,
in life,
because life doesn't have to tell you what it means
life just "is".
I wish I could fight the good fight every day,
but just as life makes us feel things—metaphors, images
so art can make us do things.
Okay,
so I can't be an angry teenager again—
everything you say is the truth, right?
So I'm this old guy,
this poet.
Well I'm not a dead poet yet!
In fact,
I'll be the poet of life!
I'll only express life
"the doing of things",
because like I said
the only real poetry is to do,
to act.
Look, I'll tell you something:
I wish I was a composer of songs,
because music is as weird and

strange, as rhythmic as life itself. Almost.
But I'm not a composer
I'm just this cranky old poet.

BOY 1 And you're not dead yet.

PASOLINI No.

BOY 1 Yeah, well I don't know what the fuck that means.

PASOLINI Neither do I. Do you want some pizza? [*to everyone on set*]
Let's all go get some pizza. And some wine. It's on me.

BOY 3 No thanks. Nothing for me.

[PASOLINI *and* BOY 1 *go off and leave* BOY 3 *alone. He puts on a sports coat and hat; he is now the* DEVIL/ANGEL, *a bourgeois Italian actor. It is later, after Pasolini's death. The* DEVIL/ANGEL *sits down and talks, fondly reminiscing about* PASOLINI]

DEVIL/ANGEL During the course of the movie, making the movie, we had this argument. [*pause*] Hah hah. [*pause*] And I asked him if he wanted to have sex with me. And he said no. I asked him that. [*pause*] I was surprised. [*he takes out a cigarette*] And then, well, what can I say, the argument that was incurred—occurred—was this. I had stipulated in my contract which involved money that I was to understand—that is to understand absolutely and exactly— what I was doing and he said, "Yes of course" or something like that. [*he imitates* PASOLINI] "Yes of course," like that. [*pause*] And it occurred to me, so I asked the question of him it occurred to me to ask, "What, if anything, is my role in the movie?" [*pause*] "What is the role I play?" [*pause*] First day, he came to me and said, "You are playing the angel." [*pause*] And I said, "Ahhh yes the angel, yes, do I have wings?" And he said, "No. This will be an angel with no wings." [*pause*] "An angel with no wings alright," I said, "I am open minded." And I was. [*pause*] And then the next day he came to me and said, "I am sorry to contradict myself." [*pause*] And I said, "Don't be, Paolo, don't be." And he said, "I am sorry but you will be playing the devil, I have changed my mind," he said "the devil". [*pause*] Of course it was all the same to me. [*pause*] "Will I have horns and a tail?" I asked. [*pause*] "No," he said. I said, "Alright," for as you well know, I am open-minded. [*pause*] And then the final day, which was the third day, [*he smokes*] Paolo came to me and said, "I have changed my mind again. You are not going to play the devil, nor are you going to play any angel at all. You are going to play the Angel of Death." "The Angel of Death," I said and smiled. [*pause*] "Do I murder people?" [*pause*] "No," he said, "you sell horses." [*pause*] "Ahhh," I said. [*pause*] And when I asked about my costume he simply grew very silent opened his eyes wide and said ... "You will appear only in the shadows which means you can be naked if you wish." [*pause*] And this comforted me somehow. [*pause*] I did not have my role, I did not have my part nor my lines nor my motivation but I knew that I would appear only in the shadows, and that I could be naked if I wished. The idea pleased me. But then again, I have always been open-minded.

[*The* DEVIL/ANGEL *smokes. Lights dim on him. Lights up on* PASOLINI *with* BOY 2. PASOLINI *is making a movie of his memory of watching movies in an open-air movie theatre. He gives the actor,* BOY 2, *some advice and then sits him down*]

PASOLINI [*setting the scene*] Impressions. Night. Rita Hayworth. South America.

[*Lights up on* RITA HAYWORTH, *dancing in a South American costume. She is singing quietly*]

[*cuing* BOY 2] An open-air movie theatre. The whispered words ...

BOY 2 Tonight. [*he whispers*] Tonight!

[BOY 1 *and* BOY 3 *run in and sit down. They yell all through the movie;* BOY 2 *is much quieter*]

BOYS [*taking lines at random*]
Wow she's a hot one, eh?
Yeah.
What tits.
Watch out ... you're shaking the whole row.
This guys pulling it so hard it's going to fall off.

Hey Luciano! She's in love with you.
How many times you gonna do it tonight?
Hey, watch out your buttons don't pop.
What a body!
What tits!
I'd like to fuck her.

[PASOLINI *goes and sits near* BOY 2]

PASOLINI   And there I was. My hands make the slow trail around the back of the chair. And he, of course, is watching Rita Hayworth. I am watching Rita Hayworth too, and she, in her South American frenzy, her Latin orgy of passion and release, gives me the courage to do what I want to do.

   BOYS   [*raising their voices*]
   Wow!
   I think I'm coming!
   Don't you know?
   Hey, Alberto, she's winking at you.
   [*they laugh*]
   Alberto's asleep!
   He doesn't know where it is.
   I'm bursting my pants.
   Shit, I'm coming. I've got the biggest dick in the world.
   No I have!
   I have!
   Alberto has!

PASOLINI   And I see suddenly that it is the right time. That now is the right time, that it is now that I must touch him, put my arm around his shoulder, that now I must risk it, Rita Hayworth wants me to risk it, the other boys, even though they don't know, they want me to risk it and I do. I let my hand fall, it falls it touches his shoulder!

   [RITA HAYWORTH'*s song builds to a furious frenzy*]

Damir Andrei as **PASOLINI** and Daniel Allman as **BOY 2** (left to right). Angelo Pedari as **BOY I** (rear)

BOYS That's it.
Shit what a mess.
I wet my pants.
I wet the whole seat.
Where's the usher?
Where's the usherette!
My dick is getting smaller now.
My dick is still hard.
Rita Hayworth makes it hard.
Alberto's never got big at all!

PASOLINI And to my surprise—to my everlasting surprise—he just simply lets his head fall. His curly head falls on my shoulder.

[**BOY 2**'s *head falls on* **PASOLINI**'s *shoulder*]

And then, in the aftermath, Rita Hayworth has calmed down somewhat, the boys are cleaning up the mess, putting their wet dicks back in their pants, he whispers ...

> BOY 1 & BOY 3
> I'm going home.
> She doesn't show her tits any more.
> What fantastic tits.
> That was fantastic.
> I could do that again.
> I could do it ten times.
> Alberto didn't do it at all.

[*Lights dim on* BOY 1, BOY 3 *and* RITA HAYWORTH]

PASOLINI He whispers ...

[*A spotlight shines on* PASOLINI *with his arm around* BOY 2]

> BOY 2 Tonight ... [*he whispers*] Tonight!

PASOLINI And my heart, not original but true ... my heart melted.

[PASOLINI *sits and smiles;* BOY 2's *head is on his shoulder.* BOY 1 *and* BOY 3 *are dimly seen leaving the theatre. Blackout. Lights up quickly on* LAURA *pacing. She is frustrated, this time because she has to do a documentary on* PASOLINI *and she doesn't know what to say. She sits. The* BOYS *watch*]

LAURA [*arguing with* PASOLINI] One could make lengthy analysis. One could analyze it to death. One could. [*pause*] Many have. [*pause*] There's the Freudian approach. Then there's the idea that I was sort of a mother figure for him or that ... yulch. I don't like it. I don't like this ... [*she gets up and shouts at* PASOLINI] kind of *analysis!* It doesn't feel right!

[*The* BOYS *smile*]

PASOLINI Keep trying. You're on the right track.
LAURA [*to crew*] He always says that, to keep me from stopping. [*she*

looks out] What particular track is that?

PASOLINI Just keep going.

LAURA Keep going. [*she sits down*] Well, there is a certain physicalness between each other. And he is very masculine and he is very ... sexy. [*she looks out*] How's that?

PASOLINI Keep going.

LAURA Yes, well. [*pause*] And he is very ... lonely. [*pause*] Not for the reasons you imagine, not *because* he is a homosexual. [*pause*] Because he is a promiscuous homosexual, perhaps. Perhaps just because he thinks about things. Perhaps because he wants things that it's not easy to ... have. Sometimes. Like a oneness with something. Perhaps. [*pause*] What now?

PASOLINI Float.

LAURA What?

PASOLINI Float now. You start to float.

LAURA Where?

PASOLINI There.

[*He points to the chair.* LAURA *climbs onto it*]

LAURA Like this?

[*She puts her arms out.* PASOLINI *removes the chair.* LAURA *floats*]

PASOLINI Yes ... just like that.

LAURA [*uncertain*] What next?

PASOLINI Now ... you sing.

LAURA But ...

PASOLINI But what?

LAURA I can't ...

PASOLINI Open your mouth.

LAURA But ...

PASOLINI Open it. Wide.

[LAURA *opens her mouth. Out of her comes a lovely singing voice. Music: something religious. As she floats and sings the* BOYS *stare at her one by one and leave.* PASOLINI *leaves.* LAURA *stares at him as he goes. The final* BOY *crosses himself. Lights dim to black*]

ACT TWO

The opening of Act Two resembles Prologue Two. This time, three mysterious figures are viewed behind the scrim. The lights come up, revealing PASOLINI *tied to a chair, and a* DOCTOR *and a* NURSE, *who seem to be torturing him*

DOCTOR The man came to me, complaining of hot rashes and a strange attraction to mud.
PASOLINI Whenever I see mud, I think of him.
DOCTOR Of hallucinations, of delusions.
PASOLINI I see him naked and I am crying, running.
DOCTOR Of an irresistible urge to drive a car.
PASOLINI The backs of heads, a turn of phrase, the way someone walks or turns or smiles all remind me of him!
DOCTOR A sad case. I administered, as best I could, a sedative.

[*The* NURSE *gives* PASOLINI *a sedative*]

PASOLINI I am slower but still I will find him. He is in my memories, in my dreams; he is in the way someone says "goodbye"; there is no compromising with him. Of course some say I am mad mad mad. I don't care.
DOCTOR He often gets in his car. And drives. The motor drowns out his cries. His cries of anguish.

[PASOLINI *screams. The* NURSE *stuffs a rag into his mouth*]

Seeing that the situation was serious, I administered two lobotomies and applied mild electric shock. Happily the treatment worked. He is now leading a normal life.

[*Music: Pop radio*]

And particularly enjoys—

[*The* NURSE *puts earphones on* PASOLINI's *head*]

AM radio stations.
PASOLINI [*lazily*] That's nice.
DOCTOR Where he used to say only "*him*" now he says only "*nice*".
Adjustment to society is complete.
PASOLINI I must have ... *nice*.

[*Pause*]

I am lonely for ... *nice*. There is nothing I would like better than
an evening with ... *nice*. I am desperately in love with *nice*. I think
nice has a nice body. Nice. Nice. Nice. Nice is better than breakfast. I want to drink my fill of nice. I must sleep with ... nice. I
am going away on vacation with nice.
DOCTOR Total recovery. Though mud still disturbs him.

[PASOLINI *wriggles to get free. The* NURSE *drips a handful of mud on
the ground*]

PASOLINI I don't think this mud is really ... *nice* ...

[*Pop radio music stops. Blackout. Lights up on a nice* BOURGEOIS
LADY *who is being interviewed about* PASOLINI's *films*]

BOURGEOIS LADY What I didn't like about the film, besides the fact
that it was so confusing, the cutting was bad, and it wasn't like the
Chaucer I knew, that I read ... [*pause*] ... just a minute ... [*to
child, off*] Take that into the kitchen will you? You're spilling it all
over. [*to audience*] He's spilling it all over. Anyway, I don't know
... I was bored, frankly, and then all that ... anal fixation thing at
the end was it ... necessary? I found it repulsive ... hold on a sec
... [*to child, off*] You're dripping it all over the floor, yes, into the
kitchen ... yes ... [*pause. To audience*] He doesn't know yet that

53

the kitchen is for eating. Anyway. I didn't like the movie. I thought it was overly long. [*pause*] Yes, that was the main problem. [*pause*] Overly long. [*she thinks for awhile*] And ... disgusting.

[*Lights dim. Lights up on* PELOSI *and the other street* BOYS *dimly viewed at the end of a long alley*]

PELOSI He's a faggot.

BOY 2 What did he do?

PELOSI Nothing. He tried. But I told him to fuck off.

BOY 3 I'd kill a faggot if he tried anything with me.

PELOSI Nino told me that they pay you fucking good money.

BOY 3 I don't want nobody's prick up my ass.

PELOSI Sometimes you don't have to let them do that.

BOY 2 No?

PELOSI They just suck you off. Just like a girl.

BOY 3 Yeah? [*pause*] Sounds sick. Makes me puke.

BOY 2 Yeah. [*pause. Shyly*] Where'd you meet him?

PELOSI In the Piazza de Cinquecento.

BOY 3 Hey ... let's go there and look at the faggots.

BOY 2 Nah.

PELOSI Yeah.

BOY 3 We're going.

BOY 2 Fucking faggots. [*he kicks a stone*]

[*Lights dim. Lights up dimly on* PASOLINI *and the* DEVIL / ANGEL *having a drink in a café-bar. The* DEVIL / ANGEL *is trying to get an acting job. During these scenes,* PASOLINI *gets more and more drunk, getting ready for his late-night prowl*]

PASOLINI You want to know? You really want to know? [*he puts down his liqueur*] First of all you must be very attractive but not with just the usual flair, you know?

DEVIL / ANGEL No, I ...

PASOLINI I will be precise. You must not be so very tall and you may be very slender. But the eyes ...

DEVIL / ANGEL [*insinuatingly*] The eyes are very important, yes?

PASOLINI Yes. Dark eyes, lit very much from within, full lips. Your hair shouldn't be too long at the back but in the front it's another story, let it fall over your eyes, so much so that sometimes you stumble and fall because you can't see where you're going ...

DEVIL/ANGEL [*laughing*] A clown.

PASOLINI In some ways, yes.

[*Pause*]

And it wouldn't be a bad thing if you were a strong boy, with all that comes with it, strong thighs that grip firmly ...

DEVIL/ANGEL It wouldn't be a bad thing?

PASOLINI No.

DEVIL/ANGEL [*suggestively*] And what would you do to me if I looked like that?

PASOLINI Unspeakable things.

[*Pause. Lights dim to black. The recorded voice of a* PEASANT WOMAN *is heard*]

> PEASANT WOMAN I was the one who found the body. We always come here on Sunday, the air she good in summer. When we get here I notice something in front of our house. I thought it was garbage and I said to my son Giancarlo, "But just look at these sons of bitches who come and throw garbage in front of the house." I went over to clean the place up and I saw it as a man's body. His head was cracked open. His hair was all smeared ... with blood.

[*Lights begin to come up dimly on* PELOSI *and* BOYS 2 & 3, *milling around the piazza in the dark*]

> He wasn't well dressed. He was lying face down with his hands under him. He had on a green sleeveless T-shirt, blue jeans dirty with grease on them, boots that came to his ankles and a brown belt. I told my husband we should go back immediately and call the police. At six-forty we were all at the police station. That's all.

[*Her voice fades out and the* BOYS *begin talking, checking out the scene. Music: Disco, faintly heard*]

PELOSI This is it?

BOY 3 Where are the faggots?

BOY 2 Shhh.

BOY 3 What?

BOY 2 They'll hear you.

PELOSI I want to get sucked off.

BOY 2 Are you crazy? Do you want to turn into a fucking faggot?

BOY 3 Who gives a fuck whether it's an ugly chick or an ugly guy?

PELOSI There's one.

BOY 3 Where?

PELOSI There. [*he points*] I've seen him before. The one behind the pillar.

BOY 2 The one with the greasy jeans?

PELOSI Yeah, and the T-shirt.

BOY 3 He's a fag?

PELOSI Yeah.

BOY 3 How do you know?

PELOSI You'll see. Just stand there.

[*They all watch the man*]

BOY 2 He looks like Jack Palance!

[*They watch*]

PELOSI He's coming this way.

BOY 2 Shhh.

[*They all act nervous and nonchalant. Blackout. The music stops. Lights up on a female* PROFESSOR]

PROFESSOR Can I say something about the Pasolini trilogy? [*pause*] Well I found them to be ... shall we say, less about Chaucer and Boccacio etcetera, then about Pasolini himself. Just as *The Gospel According to Saint Matthew* is less about Christ than about

Pasolini's communism. [*pause*] It seems a kind of a cheat, doesn't it? [*pause*] Excuse me for a moment will you? [*she leans over, raising her voice, to speak to her husband, off*] Yes ... tell them we just *can't* make it tonight, there's a staff meeting and well, yes. [*pause. To audience*] It's difficult when you're both at the same university, you have to make up double excuses for everything, anyway, yes Pasolini, yes. As an intelligent woman I would also have to say that I find his movies, frankly, offensive. They are about a male sexuality of a kind which I find horrific. They are about a male sexuality which excludes women and in fact, tenderness. It's always wrapped up with death. [*pause*] What? [*to husband, off*] No ... the wok is in the sink, dear. [*pause. To audience*] What was I saying? [*pause*] With death. And when it comes to his whole death thing well I guess my opinion is "how appropriate". If you're going to hang around with criminals how can you expect *not* to be killed? [*pause*] You will excuse me if we *don't* have dinner now we'll never make this meeting. Those are my thoughts, though I have little background in Italian literature or Pasolini. Alright?

[*The* PROFESSOR *smiles and looks off at her husband. Lights dim. Lights up on* PASOLINI *and the* DEVIL/ANGEL *in the café-bar*]

PASOLINI How's this? I am very hot, it is dark, the love surrounds me. They are joyous and they live every moment without thought, beyond discretion. They are many and it is impossible for me to love merely one.

DEVIL/ANGEL Oh no.

PASOLINI Never. They are all so different and yet the same, light or dark, large or small. When I love him it means I love ... *the world* ...

DEVIL/ANGEL [*chuckling*] The world. But ...

PASOLINI But what?

DEVIL/ANGEL Be realistic. He is not the world. He is seventeen years old and very stupid.

PASOLINI Be realistic. Is not the world seventeen years old and very stupid?

DEVIL/ANGEL Ahhh.

PASOLINI Ahhh.

DEVIL/ANGEL I get to like you more and more.
PASOLINI [*a bit unnerved by this*] You do?

[*Blackout. The recorded voice of a* RADIO REPORTER *is heard*]

RADIO REPORTER [*quoting* PELOSI's *court statement without
emotion*] Pelosi turned around and said to him "you're
crazy", that Pasolini by now was without his glasses,
which he had left in the car. And on looking him in the
face it seemed to him so much the face of a madman that
he was frightened, that he tried to run but stumbled and
fell, that he felt Pasolini on top of him hitting him on the
head with a stick—

[*Lights up, dimly, on* PELOSI, BOY 2 *and* BOY 3. *Music: "Jet Boy–Jet
Girl," Elton Motello*]

—and flung Paolo away from him, that he again started
running and again was caught and struck on the temple
and various parts of the body, that he also kicked him
once or twice in the balls, that Pasolini did not seem to
feel these kicks, that during these events he and Paolo
were alone.

[*The three* BOYS *begin speaking and milling about nervously*]

PELOSI He's coming towards us.
BOY 2 What do we say?
BOY 3 Shhh.
PELOSI Hi.

[BOY 2 *and* BOY 3 *nod in nervous assent*]

Oh ... nothing. [*pause*] Sure ... I'd like to go for a walk. [*pause*] I
dunno. [*pause*] What do you say guys?
BOY 3 Sure.
BOY 2 I ... [*pause*] Why not eh? [*pause*]
PELOSI Ostia? [*pause*] You got a car?

PASOLINI [*off-stage*] Yes.
BOY 3 Sure.
BOY 2 Sure.
PELOSI Okay.

[*They start off, except for* BOY 2]

BOY 2 No, I'm not going.
PELOSI Come on. [*he whispers*] Let's get sucked off then beat him up.
You want to?
BOY 2 Sure.

[*The three* BOYS *run off. Blackout. Music stops. Lights up on the café-bar again.* PASOLINI *is now drunk enough to be confrontational*]

PASOLINI So.
DEVIL/ANGEL So.
PASOLINI I feel as if I should ask you who you are.
DEVIL/ANGEL [*flirtatiously*] Why?
PASOLINI Because ... [*he stares at him*]
DEVIL/ANGEL Do I interest you?
PASOLINI In ... a way.
DEVIL/ANGEL What way?
PASOLINI A bad way. A boring way. [*pause*] You have bourgeois eyes.
DEVIL/ANGEL But I ... attract you?
PASOLINI In a way. [*he takes a sip of his liqueur*]
DEVIL/ANGEL Will you come home with me?
PASOLINI What's wrong with the alley?
DEVIL/ANGEL It's dirty. At home I have a comfortable bed.
PASOLINI [*removing his jacket and drunkenly standing up, angry*] I don't
like you at all!

[PASOLINI *staggers off into the night. Music: "Jet Boy–Jet Girl," Elton
Motello.* PELOSI *is dimly viewed, feeling his crotch, standing around
by a pillar.* PASOLINI *stares at him and drunkenly puts on his sunglasses. The music rises to fever pitch. Blackout. Music stops. Lights up
on a Canadian* BOURGEOIS HOMO. *He is having a drink at a bar on
Church Street in Toronto*]

BOURGEOIS HOMO Yes I saw *Teorema*. [*pause*] I thought it was *terrible*. [*pause*] So many pauses. And Terence Stamp—that may be some-body's idea of heaven but not mine—and the maid … it was silly. [*pause*] And the gay themes—again the homosexual is presented as sad and desperate. Whatever you say about *Making Love*, as a movie at least it presented … [*pause. To waiter, off*] Yes, I'll just have a Campari and soda. [*to audience*] My that is *some* waiter isn't it … so tanned, [*dismissively*] probably Key West … anyway, what-ever you say about *Making Love* as a movie it presented positive role models whereas *Teorema* was just … depressing, you know? [*his Campari is delivered*] No … lemon? Don't you have any lemon? Thanks. [*pause*] I *have* to have lemon in my Campari and … What was I saying? Depressing. Pasolini. Depressing. And I *hate* depressing.

[*Lights dim on the* BOURGEOIS HOMO *as he receives his Campari with lemon and squeals with delight. Lights up on the three* BOYS. *They are in a field. They face the audience; they are very close to the audience now*]

BOY 3 Who goes first?
BOY 2 Not me.
PELOSI I'll go first. [*stepping forward, he mimes unzipping his fly*] Suck it you faggot. Yeah suck it dry you fucking faggot. You like this don't you? Faggot. You stupid douche bag. Cuntface. You like it. Take it in your mouth and suck it dry you frigging cocksucker you. [*pause*] Hey what's the matter? [*he mimes holding his prick*] What's the matter don't you like it? [*pause*] Well I'll tell you some-thing. We don't like you. Come on guys!

[PELOSI, BOY 2 *and* BOY 3 *take a run at* PASOLINI, *who suddenly appears. There is a blinding light. All three boys climb onto* PASOLI-NI'*s body and freeze in attack positions. Lights dim on the image of* PASOLINI *with the* BOYS *stuck to him as if they were a giant insect. Lights up on* LAURA, *who is sitting on a stool*]

LAURA He was my friend. [*pause*] I had a small bench and two trees placed on the spot where he was killed. [*pause*] Someday someone

Angelo Pedari as **PELOSI** (front) and Daniel Allman as **BOY 2** (rear)

will remove them. We were friends. But because we did not have sex with each other and get married and have children we are considered strange outcasts from society. He was not that much more promiscuous than I am. And probably when I die people will say, too, "she deserved it". [*pause*] But it wasn't sex he was after, it was something else.

[*Lights up on* **PELOSI** *who is standing, bleeding slightly, in the corner*]

Some say he would have forgiven the boy if he had lived, that he would have continued on his late night ... jaunts. [*pause*] I don't know.

[*Lights up on* **PASOLINI**]

I think he would have looked at pictures of the boy from the papers, the boy with his face lightly stained with blood, and I think he would have kept the boy's picture.

[PASOLINI *walks towards* PELOSI]

His last words supposedly were "Mamma, Mamma they're killing me." He certainly loved his Mamma. And he certainly loved me. And he also loved ... them.

[LAURA *walks away. Lights dim on her.* PASOLINI *goes over and takes* PELOSI—*who now seems as docile as a child—by the hand.* PASOLINI *takes* PELOSI *centre-stage and stands looking at him. The two other* BOYS *enter and stand around* PELOSI *as* PASOLINI *speaks*]

PASOLINI I've asked him and he won't tell. He is very important ... and yet ... even wounded ... even dying ...

[BOY 2 *and* BOY 3 *pick up* PELOSI]

I have an incredible ... sympathy ... he is not someone I would like to know well. He is not ... the type. He is not one who smiles easily, in fact, you can almost never make him smile. He is not the one that you like, he is not one whom you casually see why why why?

[*Pause*]

He is not one whom ... he is not one. He is one who at that time is not watching you ... totally unself-conscious and not very nice. When he suffers, I want to hold him. It's only that. It's very simple, you see, simple.

[BOY 2 *and* BOY 3 *take* PELOSI *and raise him and cradle him in their arms*]

[*chanting*] When he suffers when he cries I will put my arm around and I will say that it is alright and I will stroke his brow and say it is alright ... and doesn't that make me some kind of a some kind of a God? I don't know, I'm not sure ... there is something I don't like, and yet ...

[BOY 2 *and* BOY 3 *bring* PELOSI *to* PASOLINI]

PASOLINI, BOY 2 & BOY 3 [*chanting together*] I am drawn to him the him that very few of you see that I have seen that he shows to me on dark steamy nights and the streetcorners and the so what that he shows himself in different guises, in different so what he plays a game so what? He is what you least expect, he is what you last want to see, he is a night last night the night before when you when you ... when you ... he is when you he is when you ...

[BOY 2 *and* BOY 3 *steal away.* PASOLINI *is left cradling the body of* PELOSI *in his arms*]

PASOLINI When you ... [*he screams*] *Ahhhhhhhhhhhhhhhhhhhhhhhhhhhhhhhhhhhh!*

[End]

THEATRELIFE

Theatrelife was first produced by Buddies in Bad Times Theatre at The Theatre Centre at the Poor Alex Theatre, 296 Brunswick Avenue, Toronto, in April 1987, with the following cast:

GEOFFREY GREGSON Graham Harley
FAY MIDDLETON Shirley Josephs
CELIA HART Ellen-Ray Hennessy
LORENZO CHIRONI Michael Caruana
TOM DELANEY Steven Walker
BRIDGET MONTCLAIR Martha Cronyn

Director: Sky Gilbert
Set and Lighting Designer: Patsy Lang
Costume Designer: Marilyn Bercovich
Stage Manager: David Pond

Characters

GEOFFREY GREGSON, the actor / manager (also plays MAJOR)
FAY MIDDLETON, the grand dame (also plays MILDRED)
CELIA HART, the bitch (also plays SYBIL)
LORENZO CHIRONI, the cad (also plays SCRUBBY)
TOM DELANEY, the ingenue (also plays CECIL)
BRIDGET MONTCLAIR, the sweet young thing (also plays GRAZIA)

Time

1983.

Setting

In the original production, the main set was GEOFFREY GREGSON's
sumptuous, Victorian-styled living-room. This cozy living-room
was complete with the *de rigueur* comfy couch, a small staircase
leading to a doorway and another door leading to the rest of the
house. A portrait of the nineteenth-century Shakespearian actor
Sir Edmund Kean loomed large over the mantlepiece. With mov-
able walls, this living-room neatly transformed into a smoking
lounge of an Edwardian ship for the play-within-the-play *Out to
Sea*. For Act Two, Scene Two, the actors stood downstage with a
railing in front of them to create the illusion that they were on the
deck of the ship.

"Vivian: When I look at a landscape I cannot help seeing all its defects. It is fortunate for us, however, that Nature is so imperfect, as otherwise we should have no art at all ....
Cyril: Well, you need not look at the landscape. You can lie on the grass and smoke and talk."

—Oscar Wilde, *The Decay of Lying*

ACT ONE, SCENE ONE

GEOFFREY GREGSON's *living-room. Music: "Violin Sonata Movement Two," Grieg. A door opens at the bottom of the stairs, shedding light into the living-room. A young man,* TOM DELANEY, *walks in. He is a blond, blue-eyed, breathtakingly beautiful ingenue*

TOM Hello? Hello? [*satisfied there is no one home, he recites in a booming theatrical voice*] How DOOO YOU DOOOOO?

[*Pause. No response. He puts down his suitcase and begins to quote from Shakespeare's* Julius Caesar]

You blocks, you stones, you worse than senseless things! O you hard hearts, you cruel men of Rome, knew you not Pompey? ... And when you saw his chariot but appear, have you not made a universal shout, that Tiber trembled underneath her banks, to hear the replication of your sounds, made in her concave shores? And do you now put on your best attire? And do you now cull out a holiday? And do you now strew flowers in his way, that comes in triumph over Pompey's blood? Be gone! Run to your houses, fall upon your knees, and pray to the Gods to intermit the plague that needs must light on this ingratitude.

[GEOFFREY GREGSON *is standing in the dark at the top of the stairs*]

GEOFFREY Excuse me.
TOM Oh. [*very nervously*] Is somebody home? I'm sorry I— I'm sorry—

[GEOFFREY *begins descending the stairs*]

GEOFFREY What is beautiful, of course, is the way that the words and images that Shakespeare uses simply *demand* that we use our voices in a certain way. If one was a rather dirty-minded scholar, one could comment on the almost sexual imagery—the chariots rushing along beside those terribly concave shores—but that would be silly. And what is most silly of all is you speaking those lines. You are far too young to play the role. The key to Marullus and Flavius is that they are very old soldiers, very old indeed. I directed it that way in Halifax and it was *most* satisfactory. At least I thought so. You are Tom. The ingenue.

TOM Yes, sir, Mr. Gregson, I'm awfully sorry ...

GEOFFREY Call me Geoffrey. And don't be sorry. It doesn't suit you. I am not at all fond of simpering ingenues.

TOM I'll never simper again.

GEOFFREY Promises. Promises.

[GEOFFREY *goes to the mantelpiece and turns on a light*]

You're early.

TOM I couldn't come on the train with the others, so I had to come by bus and the bus was earlier. I hope you don't mind.

GEOFFREY Why should I mind? It gives us a chance to talk. I can forgive anything, after all, except a lack of talent.

TOM [*nervously*] Ahhh.

GEOFFREY I think we should start off by making something very clear.

TOM Am I too early?... I wasn't sure ... that is ... coming to stay at your house ...

GEOFFREY Out-of-town actors always stay at my humble mansion. The rules are posted on the bedroom doors. [*pause*] No ... I think it important that we make something perfectly clear. In fact it is the closest thing to the truth that you will hear out of me, ever.

TOM I see.

GEOFFREY No you don't.

[*Pause*]

Pardon me. I don't know why I said that, perhaps you do see, I said it because it's an Edwardian response and we are to be performing an Edwardian play—

TOM I thought it was a hit of the twenties ...

GEOFFREY Yes, in fact it was, but most hits of the twenties, except for the inimitable Mr. Coward, were still under the Edwardian influence which means that people had interchanges such as "I see. No you don't."

TOM [*at a loss for what to say*] I ummm ... yes.

GEOFFREY So, to make a long story short, I just wanted to make it perfectly clear that you have not been invited to this theatre company—for it is a company, you must remember that, not just a group of unconnected individuals waiting for a paycheque and a call from their agent—you have been invited to this theatre company, and to be a guest in my house, not because you are so breathtakingly beautiful.

[*Pause*]

TOM [*dumbfounded*] I see.

GEOFFREY No you don't.

[*Pause*]

I really don't think that you do. Going through life as a breathtakingly beautiful adolescent can sometimes be a trial. I know. I was one once. And the most important thing to remember is that you will grow old, and because you are so lovely, it will happen suddenly, like a hurricane or a tidal wave. But enough of that. I have brought you here not because of all that, but instead because I sensed in you an indefatigable, importunate, inevitable and quite unself-conscious ability to lie.

TOM Pardon me?

GEOFFREY To lie.

TOM [*clearing his throat, not understanding at all, but not wanting to hurt* GEOFFREY'*s feelings*] Down?

GEOFFREY What?

TOM To lie ... down?

GEOFFREY [*smiling*] No. [*pause. He makes fun of* TOM *a bit*] We're off that now. We're off the beauty bit.

[*Pause*]

I am referring to your ability to lie, to create falsehood, to fabricate reality.

TOM Where do you get that idea?

GEOFFREY I know it, I sense it, I smell it. I am hardly ever wrong in these matters.

TOM I don't lie.

GEOFFREY You mustn't be offended.

TOM But aren't you calling me a liar?

GEOFFREY Yes, in a sense, but ...

[*Pause*]

TOM Are you kidding?

GEOFFREY No.

TOM Who told you I was a liar? Was it Lorenzo? That sounds like something Lorenzo might ...

GEOFFREY I have not spoken to Lorenzo since we worked together a year ago, and he is a principled young man who would not spread rumours of any kind. But you mustn't be offended. It is a compliment, coming from me. That is what theatre is all about, lying, it's what acting is all about ...

TOM Well, I don't agree.

GEOFFREY You don't?

TOM No. Acting is believing, acting is being truthful, acting is looking inside yourself to find ...

GEOFFREY Did they teach you that at theatre school?

TOM Well, yes, that's one of the ...

GEOFFREY York or Ryerson?

TOM The National Theatre School.

GEOFFREY How telling.

[*Pause*]

That's rubbish. Acting is a turn of the wrist, a batting of an eye. It's timing, it's movement, it's that crack in your voice, that quiver of your hand as you raise the cigarette to your lips. You can look inside yourself and tell the truth until you're blue in the face but the actor who excels, who truly excels—you do know the trick that Olivier had, don't you? It wasn't truth or inner understanding or emotion memory, it was that in every performance he did something that absolutely amazed the audience, that left them breathless. You must leave them breathless, my boy, and it's much more likely to be a somersault or a handstand or a tumble down three flights of steps than your inner truth.

[*Pause*]

TOM I can't honestly say that I agree.
GEOFFREY You'll change your mind. There is an actor in you. That is, a liar. It just has to be unleashed.
TOM And you will … unleash it?
GEOFFREY It's my job.
TOM And what if I don't want it to be unleashed.
GEOFFREY Well then you'll never make much of your acting or your life …

[*Pause*]

TOM [*mischievously*] After all that talk about not being hired for my pretty face, why do I feel now that you're coming on to me?
GEOFFREY Because you want me to …
TOM No I don't.
GEOFFREY See, you'll make a liar yet.

[*The sound of women's laughter*]

Well, they're here.
TOM Who?

[*The laughter gets louder*]

GEOFFREY Your fellow Thespians, your partners in crime.

[*He starts up the stairs*]

73

You will greet them for me. It's not time yet for me to make my entrance.

TOM But wait ... I don't know most of these people ...

GEOFFREY You know Lorenzo, don't you?

TOM Yes but we don't really, that is he and I ...

GEOFFREY Well you must get over it. You've heard of professionalism haven't you? Besides, it will be good lying practice for you.

[*He is almost at the top of the stairs*]

If you're at a loss for words just gossip about me ... I can hear it all now: "I just met him, he's very arrogant and enigmatic ... I'm afraid of him ... I think he hates women ... I think that being a homosexual has hurt him as a director."

[*As the noise of laughter and talking gets louder, the stage gets darker. The noise is very loud. The stage is black*]

ACT ONE, SCENE TWO

Lights up quickly and very bright. A sunlit room. It is the next morning. LORENZO CHIRONI, CELIA HART, FAY MIDDLETON, BRIDGET MONTCLAIR *and* TOM *are sitting around drinking coffee. They are in lively spirits, interrupting and talking over one another*

LORENZO I don't really think that being a homosexual has hurt his directing.

FAY I don't see what all that has to do with it at all—

BRIDGET I've heard that he doesn't like women—

CELIA That's bullshit he loves me—

BRIDGET He does?

CELIA Yeah, really. He wants to stick his finger up my twat. We've talked about it. Did I shock you Fay?

FAY No my dear, no, could I have a bit more coffee— There beside you ...

CELIA Oh yeah sorry, here I am talking about my private parts ... no really, he's a dirty old man—he likes sex—you just have to deal with him on that level ...

LORENZO There must be more to him than being a dirty old man.

FAY What is a dirty old man?

CELIA Yeah, good question.

FAY To me, it sounds pejorative, the implication being that any older person with sexual desires is dirty.

LORENZO I mean that he hires pretty boys in order to screw them. Which isn't that awful. Straight directors do the same thing with pretty girls but ...

TOM I find that remark insulting, Lorenzo.

LORENZO Well if the shoe fits ...

FAY Geoffrey Gregson is one of the most talented directors in Canada.

I can't think why he doesn't work more.

BRIDGET I'm afraid of him.

LORENZO I think it's more likely that he's afraid of you.

TOM I don't think he's afraid of anybody.

CELIA Did you all catch the rules on the bedroom doors?

BRIDGET I haven't read mine yet ...

CELIA They are an absolute hoot, I almost peed my pants. [*she takes out a piece of paper*] I ripped mine off. I just couldn't hack it. Listen: "Guests must remember that this is my home and it should be treated as such. We all must share the space which means we must have consideration for others." That's not the best. Kitchen rule number fifteen, quote: "Please remember not to use metal spatulas on Teflon pans." Unquote. Can you believe that? The man is obsessive.

FAY Great artists usually are.

BRIDGET Well I think it's wonderful of him to let us use his home like this.

CELIA Oh yeah, it's great, I just can't hack the fucking rules. I'm going to kid him about it.

BRIDGET How can you kid him—are you serious? Kid Geoffrey Gregson?

CELIA Take my advice honey, he *hates* wimpy women.

BRIDGET Are you implying that I'm wimpy?

CELIA Would you rather I came out and said it?

TOM I've heard he blocks the whole play in three days.

FAY Yes, his blocking is quite masterful. It won't seem that way at first, but later everything becomes perfectly clear.

BRIDGET I like starting with blocking.

TOM It's very old fashioned.

FAY He's an old-school director, dear. No improvisation. No theatre games.

TOM Will we do group warm-ups?

CELIA Are you kidding? Geoffrey hates physical exercise ...

LORENZO [*to* TOM] How long has it been since you graduated from the National Theatre School?

TOM A year.

LORENZO That explains a lot.

TOM Listen I ...

FAY Boys, boys.

[*A noise on the stairs*]

I think he's about to make an entrance...
BRIDGET Is it actually him?
CELIA For fuck sakes relax.
TOM And if you cast any, any ...
LORENZO "Aspersions" is the word you're looking for?
TOM On my ...
BRIDGET Shhh.

[*Pause.* GEOFFREY *enters in a dressing gown, very elegant and dramatic*]

GEOFFREY Well, you're all up.

[*He turns to* FAY]

Fay.
FAY [*getting up*] Geoffrey.

[*She hurries over and gives him a hug*]

How have you been darling?
GEOFFREY Living. Lying.

[*Pause*]

You're looking lovely.
FAY I merely grow older every year.
GEOFFREY I've let my hair go grey. Did you notice?
FAY It becomes you.
GEOFFREY Flattery will get you everywhere. And this must be ... my cast.

[*Pause*]

BRIDGET I'm Bridget Montclair.

GEOFFREY Miss Montclair. I recognize you from your photos. Your reputation precedes you.

BRIDGET It's a pleasure to be working for you Mr. Gregson.

GEOFFREY The pleasure will be mutual I'm sure. Lorenzo, how nice to see you again.

[LORENZO *and* GEOFFREY *shake hands*]

LORENZO I saw your production of *La Ronde*. It was excellent.

GEOFFREY "Excellent" I find rather boring—

LORENZO It was more than excellent it was elegant—

GEOFFREY I try to be elegant at all times. It redeems me even when I have no idea what I'm doing— Celia—

CELIA Geoffrey you fucker.

[*She gets up and hugs him*]

You look sexy as hell.

GEOFFREY I can't help it.

CELIA Still want to make a baby with a turkey baster?

GEOFFREY Please ... in front of the cast. [*he laughs*]

CELIA Oh shit if they're not used to me now ... I talk about my cunt all the time. Sorry Fay.

FAY It's alright ... is there more coffee? Oh yes, there—

GEOFFREY [*glancing at* TOM—*an afterthought*] And Tom, yes, you were here rather early. [*pause*] So.

[CELIA is *still hugging* GEOFFREY]

CELIA So ...

GEOFFREY So today is day one. I presume you've all had a look at the script. [*pause*] *Out to Sea*.

CELIA It's amazing, Geoffrey. Just fascinating.

BRIDGET I agree.

LORENZO It's a real coup, Geoffrey, discovering this lost scrap of Edwardiana ...

FAY Yes, how did you discover *Out to Sea*, Geoffrey?

TOM We're all very excited—

GEOFFREY Well it's a piece of garbage actually.

[*Pause. All look at each other.* LORENZO *clears his throat*]

CELIA Well, I thought it was pretty weird.

GEOFFREY It is very weird actually.

LORENZO The writing is not, in fact, that good.

GEOFFREY No, it isn't. But the public will like it.

FAY I agree—

TOM But surely you, that is, you didn't pick a play just because it would be a crowd-pleaser did you?

BRIDGET [*sensing that* TOM's *remark is a faux pas*] I'm sure Mr. Gregson would never do that, unless he had to pay the theatre's bills—

GEOFFREY Well it's lovely to listen to your mellifluous voices babbling on but you're missing the point.

FAY Of course dear, of course we are.

[*Uncomfortable pause*]

But what is the point darling?

LORENZO Yes. [*pause*] That is, we're all very interested in the play, we think it's a bold choice, but we wonder why—

GEOFFREY You're wondering why I chose this fascinating scrap of Edwardiana, well let me tell you it's a lovely piece of garbage and lovely garbage is sometimes more interesting than a lovely master-piece because it's all involved with artifice actually and because it was written to please a public and also to compliment a public on it's intelligence—

LORENZO How true—

GEOFFREY Yes and it's also very interesting because it's about death, a peculiarly Victorian concern and of course in our culture death is ignored, it's too unpleasant—

LORENZO That's so true Geoffrey, whenever I watch TV and one of those ads for starving children—Feed the Children—comes on, I always watch it just to force myself to confront—

GEOFFREY Well I never watch TV—

LORENZO Well I don't usually—

CELIA I think the play is fucking good, I don't care what you say, Geoffrey.

GEOFFREY You don't, do you?

CELIA And there's a fucking good part in it for me, I get to play a real bitch and I'm going to steal the show.

GEOFFREY If I were you, Bridget, I wouldn't stand for that.

BRIDGET No, I won't. You just watch it, Celia.

CELIA Fuck off, wimp.

GEOFFREY So. [*pause*] I think I'll just be getting ready. We'll see you all there at one. Explore the town. Get to know the dreadfully middle-class residents of scenic Regina.

FAY It's a reading at one isn't it? No marching around?

GEOFFREY No marching around today—

TOM So we don't need to wear rehearsal clothes.

GEOFFREY No. [*pause*] I personally won't be bothered if you wear nothing at all.

TOM I see.

GEOFFREY No you don't.

[*Pause*]

Good day all.

[*He goes towards the stairs*]

Don't be late. I punish lateness with bad blocking. You'll be forced to light cigarettes, talk and make love all at the same time.

[*He is at the point of disappearing*]

A difficult if rather too realistic proposition.

CELIA What an amazing bugger.

FAY Yes he is, rather.

CELIA I'd love to have his baby.

LORENZO I think at the rate we're going Tom is a lot more likely to have it than you Celia.

TOM Listen Lorenzo—

LORENZO I'm listening—

TOM Even if he does have a thing for me, which I'm sure he doesn't—

LORENZO What was all that stuff about [*he imitates* GEOFFREY] "I personally won't be bothered if you wear nothing at all— I see— No you don't"?

TOM It's sort of a private joke, you wouldn't understand.

LORENZO A private joke eh—we're already at the private-joke stage, we've skipped stage one, we've skipped orders you around or ignores you and we're already at private jokes—

FAY Lorenzo please—

LORENZO What?

FAY This is so ... indelicate not to mention downright rude—

LORENZO Well I've seen it happen in too many productions. Geoffrey gets infatuated with the male ingenue and the male ingenue turns out to be straight or not into older men and Geoffrey just gets so cranky! Well all I can say is, Tom, if you're not going to sleep with him then be fair to all of us and tell him the truth right away.

TOM But the one thing he said he didn't want from me was the truth.

CELIA That's just Geoffrey trying to sound deep. The fact is he's got a dick like everybody else.

[*Pause*]

I mean every other guy.

[*Pause*]

Sorry Fay.

FAY No darling please don't be inhibited because I'm a bit old fashioned. Is the coffee cold?

[*Lights dim*]

BRIDGET Well I'm just terrified—

CELIA There's nothing to be scared of little girl. His bark is worse than his bite.

BRIDGET It's not that that scares me, it's the play.

FAY Oh yes, the play. It is a bit odd.

LORENZO Irrelevant if you ask me.

CELIA I like it. I don't think anybody else will.

TOM Why did he choose *Out to Sea*? I didn't understand.

LORENZO Ask him, maybe he'll *explain* it to you *privately*.

BRIDGET And my part ... it's so large—

CELIA That's nothing to be afraid of honey. Any lines you don't like just give them to me. Just don't start breaking down in tears a week from opening. I couldn't hack it.

[*Lights dim*]

ACT ONE, SCENE THREE

The sound of a woman weeping. Lights up on BRIDGET *and* FAY *sitting together.* BRIDGET *is crying as* FAY *comforts her*

BRIDGET And there's only a week left, just a week—

FAY It's alright dear, a week is a long time—

BRIDGET But it's mostly technical, he even warned us that after tomorrow there won't be much time for acting.

FAY Oh you'd be surprised how one can use those technical rehearsals for acting practice if one is really crafty.

BRIDGET But I don't ... I don't know what I'm doing, I have no idea why I'm really up there ...

FAY Well maybe you should ask him about it—

BRIDGET But I have, I ask him endlessly, we have these little meetings and talks but I know he's getting tired of them, and I know he's getting tired of me—

FAY Geoffrey is really very patient.

[*Pause*]

Do you mind if I ask you something?

BRIDGET Well ... no, not at all, if it will help. [*she sniffles*]

FAY Darling now first of all you must remember that you are very talented. You've got *it*. Of course you have. I don't tell people they've got *it* if they haven't. I tell them to take up another line of work.

BRIDGET How do you know that I have *it?*

FAY Well one just knows these things, that's all, it's like being in love, you just know and you can't explain why. Now ... you must tell me—most of your experience is in that, what is it ... that little theatre in Toronto?

BRIDGET [*through tears*] Theatre Passe Muraille—

FAY Yes, it sounds like a lovely little theatre but, let me ask … do they have sets and doors that open and things like that?

BRIDGET Well, sometimes, but not usually, usually there's not enough money and you have to mime the doors and things—

FAY Well, first of all, there you are, just having to deal with all the trappings of a real theatre, that is, a larger theatre, with real walls and doors and, well, the other thing— Most of the time haven't you been playing girls who are close to your own age and experience?

BRIDGET Well yes, sort of—

FAY Yes, of course, young modern girls, but in this play, you are portraying almost a spirit of a girl, and on top of that, the spirit of a late Edwardian girl—

BRIDGET [*getting up restlessly*] Oh I'm so tired of people telling me that the problem is I've never been in a period play— You know it may not be old plays we do in Toronto but it's still theatre—

FAY Yes of course it is, no one is saying it isn't—

BRIDGET Because everybody is always telling me that I've never done it before and it doesn't make me feel very confident because I have done it, I have acted—

FAY But this is a different kind of acting, and what we're trying to tell you is that it's perfectly reasonable that you'll have some difficulty, perfectly normal, but you'll be fine once you relax, you work too hard anyway, you work very hard—

BRIDGET I don't work hard enough—

FAY I've never seen anyone work like you—

BRIDGET Really?

FAY Honestly.

BRIDGET But he's not satisfied.

FAY How do you know dear?

BRIDGET Because he's so fidgety around me—

FAY That's Geoffrey, he's a very odd man, and just between you and me, though I love him dearly, and he is *very* talented, he's *always* acting.

BRIDGET But that's not the way directors are supposed to be. I mean they're supposed to be honest, you're supposed to trust them—

FAY Well Geoffrey is honest, in a dishonest way, it's very hard to

explain, would it help you, maybe it would, to understand
Geoffrey to know that he and I were ... what's the modern term
for it? We were ... now this is many years ago when we were ado-
lescents—close to your age actually—we were lovers once.

FAY [*astonished*] You and *Geoffrey?*

FAY Yes.

BRIDGET But that's impossible! He's a—

FAY Well he wasn't then. Or at least he was pretending he wasn't.
Geoffrey loves games. He loves them even more than life itself,
playing, play-acting, which is why he is such a marvellous actor
when he gets onstage, and you know, just between you and me, I
sometimes wonder if he's really a ... a you know—

BRIDGET You don't think he's a—you know?

FAY Well I wonder—

BRIDGET But he's after Tom—

FAY Yes, but—

BRIDGET But he's the most famous—you know—in Canada—

FAY Yes, all that is true, but sometimes I think he just likes all the theatricality of being a—you know—even more than the actual ...
um ... whatever.

BRIDGET Now I'm very confused. I thought maybe he hated
women—

FAY Well that is not true at all, he's particularly fond of the more
vocal—

BRIDGET You mean loud obnoxious filthy mouths like Celia?

FAY Well, I didn't want to say—

BRIDGET But that's what she is—and *she* doesn't help any—every time
I flub a line she always says, "Got too many honey give one to
me." I could kill her—

FAY You have to learn to understand Celia too. She *also* is a very good
actress—I sometimes think she's a little less foul in her personal
life than she pretends to be.

BRIDGET But I don't understand. It's almost as if you're saying that to
be a good actress you have to be totally fake all the time—

FAY No, I'm not saying that really—

BRIDGET Now I'm even more confused. [*she seems about to cry again*]

FAY Wait, I think he's descending the stairs. Do you want me to stay?

BRIDGET Oh please don't leave me alone with him, he scares me to death—

FAY Well here he is now, I'll just stay and listen in then—

[GEOFFREY *enters in a dressing gown*]

GEOFFREY Ahhh yes Bridget. You wanted to talk. [*he sees* FAY] Fay dear.

FAY Darling.

GEOFFREY I can't imagine why Fay can't solve your problem for you. She's so good at solving things ... Call me Geoffrey.

BRIDGET [*saying the word tentatively*] Geoffrey. I want to tell you, first of all, how much I'm enjoying working on this play and working with you—

GEOFFREY Yes, yes, let's get through with all that. Now what's bothering you today?

BRIDGET Well ... it's my big speech.

GEOFFREY Ahhh ... the big speech. Well it wouldn't be your little speech, would it?

BRIDGET No, it's the big symbolic one that I don't—

GEOFFREY Well, do tell me, what methods have you been using to attack it?

BRIDGET Well, I, that is—

GEOFFREY What I want to know is, what have you been writing down in your little notebook, the one you bring to rehearsals—

BRIDGET Oh that ... well a lot of analysis of reasons why she doesn't want to marry him—

GEOFFREY Why don't you think she wants to marry him?

BRIDGET Oh ... lots of reasons, because he doesn't seem too bright, because he's over-concerned about her, really, I think because she's had such over-protective parents she—

GEOFFREY Excuse me dear, but you must realize that this play is, to all intents and purposes, pre-Freud.

BRIDGET Well it *was* written in the twenties—that is I don't mean—

GEOFFREY Yes, but the psychology, or lack of it, is purely Edwardian.

BRIDGET Everybody keeps saying that and I don't know what it means—

GEOFFREY Well, the first thing it means, of course, is that the words are no more than that sometimes, they are just words. Now why

86

don't you just try your speech for me right now. Fay, do you have a script?

FAY Yes darling.

GEOFFREY And, Fay will do the boyfriend's little ... interjections.

[FAY *moves to the shadowy sidelines of the room*]

Now when you say the speech I don't want you to think about anything at all, do you hear me?

BRIDGET But—

GEOFFREY Quiet, now, I just want you to say the words clearly, enunciate very precisely, let the words flow gently.

BRIDGET That's all?

GEOFFREY Yes—

BRIDGET But—

GEOFFREY Try it. You'll discover something. I guarantee it. Try.

[BRIDGET *clears her throat. Pause*]

BRIDGET Don't you see? I'm not ready.

FAY [*from the shadows*] Why Grazia?

BRIDGET Because life is too ... there's a kind of happiness I want to find first, if I can—

FAY Aren't you happy with me?

BRIDGET Yes dear, but that isn't quite what I mean ... I wish I knew how to tell you. There's something out there that I must find first. Something I must ... understand ...

FAY May I go with you?

BRIDGET I'd rather be alone if you ... don't mind ...

[*She stands quietly looking out*]

Well?

GEOFFREY Now *that* was very interesting. Much more interesting than what you've done before.

BRIDGET You think so?

GEOFFREY Oh yes. Wasn't it Fay?

FAY Oh yes.

[*Pause*]

BRIDGET But it felt ... fake.

GEOFFREY But the theatre is fakery, trumpery. It's all a sham, it steals your heart for the price of a ticket, you know that. And you must steal the audience's heart, my dear—

BRIDGET But what about truth, what about the inner truth of the scene, you see we've never really talked about—

GEOFFREY Well the inner truth, of course, is that she is a little in love with death.

BRIDGET In love with death?

GEOFFREY Yes.

BRIDGET But how can someone be in love with death?

GEOFFREY Oh very easily. He's a handsome one, death is.

BRIDGET Is it like being in love with a dying man?

GEOFFREY It might be, though it's a bit more like meeting death one day, on the patio, and he's wearing a neatly pressed pair of trousers and a smart tuxedo jacket and you can't help it [*acting now*] because you find death so unbearably funny, he is so witty, death, that he almost makes you laugh.

BRIDGET Does death make you laugh?

GEOFFREY Every time I think about it. The concept that I have ever lived I find even funnier. Come now, see him dear, greet him, he's as handsome as Tom and as high-minded as Lorenzo and wittier even than I.

BRIDGET But I can't laugh, I can't—

GEOFFREY [*in a stage whisper*] Quick, you see him, he beguiles you, he hypnotizes you, he's not what you expected, he defies description— Speak my dear— Speak—

BRIDGET [*carefully*] Don't you see I'm not ready?

FAY [*lowering her voice*] Why Grazia?

BRIDGET Because life is too ... there's a kind of happiness I want to find first if I can.

FAY Aren't you happy with me?

BRIDGET Yes dear, but that isn't quite what I mean ... I wish I knew how to tell you— [*she seems transfixed*]

[TOM *quietly enters the room and watches the scene from the shadows*]

There's something out there I must find first. Something that I
must ... understand ...

TOM & FAY [*simultaneously*] May I go with you?

[*A strange spell has fallen over the room*]

BRIDGET [*turning to* TOM] Yes. Yes ... you may.

[*Pause*]

I'm sorry.

[*Pause*]

Because of the way you described death it's almost as if ... suddenly when Tom came in, it's as if Tom was ... death—

TOM What's this?

GEOFFREY Tom, death. How incongruous.

TOM What's going on?

GEOFFREY An acting lesson. It's over now. You've about got it. There
was some tremendous lying going on there that time. Lying with a
vengeance.

BRIDGET Yes, I felt it too.

[*She grabs* TOM]

Tom, come with me. I want to go over the scene. Thank you ...
Geoffrey. Thank you.

GEOFFREY You're very welcome.

[*Pause.* BRIDGET *and* TOM *start to leave.* FAY *remains in the shadows*]

TOM But—

[*Giggling,* BRIDGET *pulls* TOM *off the stage with her*]

FAY [*pause*] So ... are you in love with him?

[*Silence*]

Are you fatally infatuated with him?

GEOFFREY It's quite fatal. This death I shall enjoy.

FAY But he's quite nothing isn't he? Simply—lovely?

GEOFFREY Oh no, he's much more than that. I think there's an actor there.

FAY Those words—I've heard them before—

GEOFFREY Yes, you have.

[*Pause*]

No ... the innocence—the sweet doe-eyed innocence is all an act.

FAY It is?

GEOFFREY Oh yes. That boy could teach me a thing or two about love.

FAY How strange. I never would have seen that.

GEOFFREY But then ... you're not really interested are you?

FAY [*laughing slightly*] Not really, Geoffrey.

[FAY *and* GEOFFREY *sit down together*]

GEOFFREY Darling.

FAY Dearest.

[*They kiss. Pause*]

GEOFFREY No, he's been a very bad boy, and he's pretending that he's all Wonderbread and my favourite things, but he's been very bad and if he's this good at acting like a good boy, imagine how he would excel at acting truly bad!

FAY The mind boggles. But you must tell me a little more about this obsession with death. I notice all your work in this play seems to centre around that topic.

GEOFFREY Yes, death ... sickness ... illness ... let's talk about that ...

[*Lights dim*]

Lights come up on CELIA, *centrestage, and* LORENZO, *in the corner, smoking. They are arguing*

CELIA Death sickness illness! I'm tired of that crap! This play is so depressing. We have the evening off—let's go to a movie let's go see some Hollywood schlock, I mean Sally Field must be tilling a farm somewhere and holding her own against the locusts, I need that, or let's watch TV let's just let loose—

LORENZO I *have* to talk to you about this.

CELIA Oh Lori you can be such a bore sometimes. Hasn't anybody ever told you that?

LORENZO [*really angry*] Fuck off Celia, just fuck off!

CELIA Don't use that booming anger that gets you so many disaffected-young-man parts. Lori look, I'm sorry but I don't want to sit around and listen to your complaints tonight. What is it now, your costume is it? Fay forgetting her lines? We all know that the dressing rooms don't have showers; so this isn't the National Arts Centre, not every theatre in Canada can be the National Arts Centre, this is Saskatchewan and wheat money built this theatre and this year it was a bad year for wheat—

LORENZO Celia listen—

CELIA I'll listen if you promise me that it's not a complaint—no more bullshit, *Mona.* You know the crew nicknamed you *Mona*—

LORENZO It's not a complaint, it's a worry—it's not bullshit, it's life and death—

CELIA Oh life and death I get enough of that in the fucking newspapers—have you picked one up lately? There is nothing that doesn't kill you, food, sex, TV, clothes, well let me tell you I'm going to spend the next ten years fucking, eating, watching schlock and

wearing polyester and if it kills me I'll die happy—
LORENZO What about AIDS then?
CELIA What about what?
LORENZO AIDS. The disease.
CELIA Yeah.

[*Pause*]

What about it?

[*Pause*]

That's what I'm talking about. But I probably won't get it because I really don't fuck around that much and hardly ever bisexuals. There was Nigel, but he wouldn't have had it. Anyway they say the AIDS virus isn't very happy in cunts thank God.

[*Pause*]

LORENZO In this specific instance, I wasn't referring to you. Could we just get off of Celia for a minute, get off the Celia express just momentarily.
CELIA [*offended*] Well.
LORENZO I'm talking about AIDS and I'm talking about a very real fear.

[*Pause*]

You've been watching this obsession that has slowly been developing between Geoffrey and Tom.

[CELIA *nods*]

Celia, you *can* talk.

[*She shakes her head*]

Fuck off you cunt.

CELIA Fuck off you prick.

LORENZO I knew I could get you to talk. Now, have you observed this—

CELIA [*imitating him*] Yes I've observed this—

LORENZO This obsession that Geoffrey has for Tom.

CELIA And you don't approve.

LORENZO It's not a matter of approving or disapproving. It's a matter of being concerned for Geoffrey's—well, his own life, that's all. And Tom's as well.

CELIA What are you talking about?

LORENZO Alright I'll just tell you then. I just hope you can take it seriously for once, show a little human feeling.

CELIA [*annoyed*] Lori—

LORENZO Tom has AIDS.

CELIA What?

LORENZO Tom has AIDS.

CELIA That's impossible.

LORENZO Why?

CELIA Because ... well it's just ...

[*Pause*]

How do you know?

LORENZO He told me.

CELIA When?

LORENZO When we were working in Toronto. It was just when he had the tests and he was very upset about it and we went out drinking and he told me.

CELIA Tom is ... dying?

LORENZO Well no. Not exactly.

CELIA But I thought you said—

LORENZO Well apparently he has the HIV virus, I don't know if he's actually sick—

CELIA So you're afraid he's going to give it to Geoffrey?

LORENZO Yes, to put it baldly, yes.

CELIA Did it ever occur to you that all of this was none of your fucking business?

LORENZO You may not think it is, but I happen to love Geoffrey and I don't want to see him die. I also don't think it's good for Tom to act like this, it's as if he's deluding—

CELIA You happen to love Geoffrey?

LORENZO Yes.

CELIA That is the biggest crock of bullshit I ever heard.

LORENZO Celia I don't see how you're qualified—

CELIA He's the *only* director who can work with you. He's the only one who will hire you more than once. You are a load of trouble, Lori, you and I both know that and the only reason you "love" Geoffrey is because he is willing to give you a regular job—

LORENZO I have a great deal of respect for the man's work—

CELIA For his work? You don't know anything about his work—his work has to do with real human feeling, with issues of life and death. You're so wrapped up in your own selfish little knot of career management you wouldn't know human feeling if you fell over it. And you don't even like faggots!

LORENZO I didn't used to like faggots, Celia. Now I understand they're just like us. It was meeting great and fascinating gay men like Geoffrey that turned me around. It's just this tragic AIDS. I can understand when sometimes an outsider can help them to see things more rationally—

CELIA You make me sick you really do. You *are aware* I suppose that they will be, presumably, having safe sex?

LORENZO Well Celia I don't know ... that is ... is sex ever really safe ... for them?

CELIA You make me sick, you really do. Your problem is, you just don't have a dick, that's all you are dick*less* and you just can't handle it that faggots for the most part are actually interested in sex whereas your dick withered away long ago.

[LORENZO *grabs her*]

LORENZO Hey.

[*He kisses her hard on the lips*]

There, how's that? You think I'm dickless eh?

[*He presses up against her*]

Well what's that? What do you call that—
CELIA [*intense, frightened*] Let go of me, Lorenzo. [*her voice builds*] I said ... let go!

[*She pushes him off*]

LORENZO For a girl who talks about her cunt so much your legs sure are glued together.
CELIA Oh grow up.

[*She goes to the door*]

And keep your untalented prurient little nose out of Geoffrey's business. Geoffrey and Tom should be able to manage their own lives better than someone who's never graduated from emotional kindergarten— Screw off—

[*She goes to exit*]

LORENZO I'm going to tell him.
CELIA Oh please.

[*She exits*]

LORENZO I have to tell him. Tomorrow. After the dress rehearsal. I have to tell him.

[*Lights dim*]

ACT ONE, SCENE FIVE

Music: theme from Magnificent Obsession. *Lights come up on the play* Out to Sea.
It is the smoking lounge of a luxury liner, 1923. The passengers are travelling aboard a ship but they do not know why. The "actors" all play passengers except for LORENZO *who plays* SCRUBBY, *the Cockney steward.*
The curtain rises on the last scene in Act Two of Out to Sea *as* MILDRED *consoles* GRAZIA

GRAZIA [*weeping*] But you see ... I have to tell him ...
MILDRED Tell him what?
GRAZIA The truth.
MILDRED What is the truth?
GRAZIA That's just it ... I don't know ...
MILDRED Well Cecil is a very nice young man, I'm sure he won't mind putting off the engagement—that is, how long were you thinking?
GRAZIA [*gazing off*] Oh ... forever ...
MILDRED Forever is a long time. Aren't you fond of him?
GRAZIA Yes, I'm fond of him. But one doesn't build one's life on fond, does one?
MILDRED Married lives have been built on less lasting emotions than fondness.
GRAZIA Oh ...
MILDRED Kindness, a mutual respect, a shared affinity for certain outdoor sports—

[SCRUBBY *enters*]

96

SCRUBBY I brought your sherry mum.

MILDRED Oh thank you, Steward.

SCRUBBY Call me Scrubby mum.

MILDRED Well, Scrubby then.

SCRUBBY [*to* GRAZIA] Are you certain you wouldn't like a bit of sherry mum? It makes the cruise ever so much smoother.

[GRAZIA *turns on* SCRUBBY *suddenly and grabs him savagely*]

GRAZIA Tell me— You must tell me where this ship is going. Where are we headed? Where where where?

SCRUBBY Why I'm sure mum, if you don't know, I certainly couldn't tell you.

[*He leaves*]

GRAZIA Oh ... it's so frustrating. [*pause*] Don't you ever wonder where we're going?

MILDRED Oh I never wonder dear, I never give it a thought. I just go along for the ride. I bought my ticket to anywhere and that's where I'd like to go. It suits me fine.

[SYBIL *enters, on the arm of the* MAJOR]

MAJOR That's jolly good, that is, you really told him off! Jolly right you did too. [*he laughs*]

SYBIL Well, I just said prince or no prince I don't want your diamonds or your pearls I want your love, and he wasn't willing to give me that. He did own such an awful lot of diamonds and pearls though. [*greeting them*] Grazia darling. How are you?

GRAZIA Do you really want to know?

SYBIL Of course I do, dear. I've just been telling the Major here all about how I refused to marry Prince Caspian of Bulgaria because he offered me too many diamonds.

GRAZIA [*bitterly*] Can there ever be too many diamonds?

SYBIL But, my dear, a diamond without love is like a horse without a saddle. It would be quite naked—

MAJOR [*chuckling*] Jolly right, m'dear, you have a way with words—

doesn't she? And pretty as a picture too—

GRAZIA [*breaking through the levity*] How can you be jolly? How can any of you be jolly when you don't know why we're here, what we're doing on this ship?

MAJOR It's best not to bother about the why and wherefore of things—I paid my dues. The Crimean War, the Boers, those dirty dogs—and I think I deserve something, a nice cruise is fine—

SYBIL I agree. Don't look a gift horse in the mouth my dear. Your ticket was paid for wasn't it?

GRAZIA Yes, but—

SYBIL Then that's all you should worry about.

GRAZIA All the same I can't help wondering—

[CECIL *enters*]

CECIL Grazia.

[CECIL *and* GRAZIA *go to each other. They hold hands and gaze into each other's eyes*]

MILDRED Aren't they pretty as a picture?

SYBIL I find them pretty appalling.

GRAZIA Cecil.

CECIL Shhh. Well everyone. I've decided that tonight's the night I'm going to pop the question and I want you all to be witnesses. Grazia darling, I'm going down on my knees. I love you, more than the sun, more than the moon, I love you more than my own life, and I want you to marry me. What do you say darling? Is it yes? It must be.

GRAZIA Oh.

[*Music: theme from* Magnificent Obsession. GRAZIA *looks off into the distance. All watch, rapt, except for* SYBIL, *who plays with the train of her dress*]

MAJOR My dear, it's only a question of making up your mind.

GRAZIA [*to* CECIL] You know I love you and I want to please you. I ... Don't you see? I'm not ready.

Steven Walker as CECIL, Ellen-Ray Hennessy as SYBIL, Graham Harley as MAJOR, Martha Cronyn as GRAZIA, Shirley Josephs as MILDRED, and Michael Caruana as SCRUBBY (left to right)

CECIL But why, Grazia—

GRAZIA Because life is too … [*she looks off*] There's a kind of happiness I want to find first, if I can.

CECIL Aren't you happy with me?

GRAZIA Yes dear, but that isn't quite what I mean … I wish I knew how to tell you. There's something out there that I must find first. Something that I must … understand …

[GRAZIA *moves away from* CECIL. *He goes to her*]

CECIL May I go with you?

GRAZIA I'd rather be alone if you don't mind.

[*The music swells.* GRAZIA *disappears out the door. Pause*]

SYBIL Well what, may I ask, was that all about?

MILDRED She's young, romantic—

SYBIL She's out of her mind. [*pause*] Listen here Cecil, if it's a good time you want why don't you marry me? I'll know how to spend your money and what to say at parties and I don't know quite what else a wife is for.

MAJOR Well I'll be ... you were talking of love before—

SYBIL That was love, this is marriage. The two are quite incompatible.

CECIL But of course I love Grazia. I must marry *her*.

SYBIL Well. Then I'm not staying down here in this gloomy old smoking room. Why don't we go out on deck and gaze at the moon?

MAJOR I think I can be persuaded.

SYBIL What about you Mildred?

MILDRED I'd love to dear. If it's a slip of a moon I can think back to being a slip of a girl, which was many years ago.

CECIL I'll come along too. Maybe it will clear my head. It's filled with anguish and confusion at the moment.

SYBIL To the upper deck. To life! Let Grazia drown in her morbid fantasies. We'll have a party!

[*They all move off, talking amongst themselves. Pause. Music: theme from* Magnificent Obsession. SCRUBBY *enters with his tray*]

SCRUBBY Hello? Nobody there? Where have they all gone? Oh blimey they've left their sherry behind. They're a heedless lot and thankless too. But wots a body to do? Wots a body to do ...

[GRAZIA *enters at the back and lingers, sadly. She slowly walks over to* SCRUBBY]

GRAZIA [*frightened and intense*] Scrubby— Oh!

SCRUBBY [*startled*] Blimey but you put the fear of God in me ma'am.

GRAZIA [*slowly*] Well that shouldn't be any problem for you, should it?

SCRUBBY Why I don't know what you mean, mum.

GRAZIA Why I think you do, Scrubby, I think you do. You're on personal terms with God, aren't you?

[*Pause. The lights begin to dim*]

SCRUBBY Why, I can assure you, mum, God and me we've never spoke a word.

GRAZIA That's very odd. Then there's a messenger through which he speaks to you?

SCRUBBY Are you alright mum? You look a bit peaked around the edges—

GRAZIA Yes I'm alright, more alright than I've been in my life. Tell me. You're the ferryman aren't you? Charon, the ferryman of the Styx.

SCRUBBY The only sticks I know about mum is the ones we use to stir the cocktails, or the toothpicks the Major likes after dinner to clean his—

GRAZIA We are—now answer me truthfully—we are all ... dead aren't we? All the passengers on this ship?

[*Pause*]

SCRUBBY Why, er, ahhh ... yes ma'am. Yes we are all dead. [*chuckles*] They don't find out so soon as you have as a rule. But wots a body to do. [*pause*] Wots a body to die.

[*Pause*]

Oh dear ...

[SCRUBBY *goes out mumbling as* GRAZIA *gazes after him. Blackout*]

ACT TWO, SCENE ONE

It's late at night after the dress rehearsal. Lights are low. LORENZO *is sitting in the corner in the dark, drinking.* GEOFFREY *stands with a drink in his hand. Music: something classical*

GEOFFREY [*laughing*] Wots a body to die …

LORENZO [*laughing too*] Well … it's logical … it's a flub, but it's logical.

GEOFFREY Yes I suppose it is …

LORENZO I am the symbol … as it were, of death …

GEOFFREY The symbol of death. What's happened to that wonderful custom these days?

LORENZO Why what do you mean?

GEOFFREY I mean that in the nineteenth century characters were named Death, someone had to play the character of Death or Joy, or in Maeterlinck the Spirit of Love or the Blue Bird of Happiness—why is theatre so hampered? What has happened to our ability to dream to believe … I suppose it's all gone into the movies—

LORENZO Special effects—

GEOFFREY Yes but I'm talking about the period where special effects, the technical wizardry, all happened in the mind, which of course makes me old fashioned—

LORENZO No, Geoffrey, no. I hope you won't think I'm flattering you when I say your direction of *Out to Sea* is a work of genius.

GEOFFREY Well—

LORENZO No Geoffrey—I don't know if the critics will see it, they are so dense—but it will still be there, a stillness, a quality of lyricism, of haunting fear, of anguish.

[*Pause*]

GEOFFREY Well, we'll find out tomorrow won't we? Tomorrow's the big night.

LORENZO Yes. [*pause*] Geoffrey?

GEOFFREY [*drinking*] Hmmm.

LORENZO I've been meaning to discuss something with you that's on my mind—

GEOFFREY I hope it's not acting, you're doing a lovely job, you know that, Scrubby is a little gem—

LORENZO Well, thank you, no, I just do my job. It's more—and I don't mean to pry but I'm concerned—it's more … personal.

GEOFFREY Personal.

[*Pause*]

But you and I never get personal, Lori.

LORENZO I know. And I want to change all that, because I'm concerned about you, very concerned.

GEOFFREY Dear me, am I drinking too much? Am I becoming over-indulgent as a director? You must tell me.

LORENZO It's about Tom.

[*Pause*]

GEOFFREY What about Tom?

LORENZO It's about what I've been observing between you and Tom.

[*Pause*]

GEOFFREY I don't know if I like the sound of this.

LORENZO Well you might not but I think it's time that someone talked to you, for your own good.

GEOFFREY For my own good.

[*Pause*]

I am not at all used to being treated like a little boy, Lorenzo.

LORENZO I know. But I think for once you need to be.

GEOFFREY How terribly melodramatic.

LORENZO The situation is melodramatic, I admit. [*pause*] Have you slept with him yet?

GEOFFREY Lorenzo please. [*pause*] I really don't see that *that* is any of your business.

LORENZO You'll be sorry Geoffrey if you don't tell me before I tell you what I have to tell you.

GEOFFREY You know, I once told Fay that the reason I was a homosexual had nothing to do with lovely young men and everything to do with being theatrical. If I was a heterosexual I doubt that anyone would ever talk to me in such an overblown and nineteenth-century fashion. You've started off sounding like a character from Ibsen, now you're moving closer to Alexandre Dumas. It's retrogressive in terms of theatrical history but nevertheless delightful.

LORENZO I wish you wouldn't turn everything into a play all the time.

GEOFFREY But we are in a play aren't we? Well, aren't we? Isn't there an audience out there?

[*He points to the audience*]

Look.

LORENZO [*glancing, guilty*] No there isn't, of course there isn't.

GEOFFREY Oh but you sense that there is. "All the worlds a—" to quote the Bard. And you are playing to the balcony, Lorenzo, you are playing to the balcony. Now I must know I simply must know what your guilty secret is.

LORENZO It's not mine. It's Tom's.

GEOFFREY Tom's. I see.

LORENZO No you don't.

GEOFFREY Now we've moved to Somerset Maugham, I'm all ears.

LORENZO Well then you've forced me to tell you bluntly and so I won't ... mince words. It's for your own good Geoffrey and because I love you. I didn't used to understand about this gay business, but now I can say honestly that my best friends are—it's just when any lifestyle gets dangerous for the participants, I get concerned. I happen to think you are a delightful, charming and above all talented person and I don't like to see you destroying yourself. And I don't want to see Tom—deluding himself.

GEOFFREY [*watching* LORENZO, *bewitched*] Go on.

LORENZO Well since you've forced me to just tell you and you won't tell me if you've slept with him or not I'm going to tell you something I should have told you a long time ago, and I don't care if it's none of my business, I care about you. Tom has AIDS.

GEOFFREY [*unruffled*] Hmmm.

LORENZO What?

GEOFFREY [*calculatingly*] I said—

[*Pause*]

Hmmm.

[*Pause*]

How do you know this?

LORENZO He told me.

GEOFFREY When?

LORENZO In Toronto. When we were doing the show at Toronto Free Theatre—

GEOFFREY Oh, yes, the *Othello* with all that dreadful incidental music. I remember.

[*Pause*]

How long does he have?

LORENZO Well if I can believe what Tom told me, and I'm not sure that I can, he basically has HIV and no symptoms yet—

[*Pause*]

So.

[*He waits*]

Aren't you upset?

GEOFFREY Ummm.

[*Pause*]

No. I can't say that I am.

[*Pause*]

LORENZO But I thought you were in love with him?
GEOFFREY I don't know if it's love really. Passionate infatuation.

[*Pause*]

I think, actually, that I'd just like to have a conversation with him
with his clothes off.

[*Pause*]

I don't know what one calls that really.

[*Pause*]

Intellectual nudity?
LORENZO But Geoffrey I can't believe that you're not perturbed by this
news at all, I mean—
GEOFFREY Lori, Lori, Lori. Poor dear Mona Chironi. That's what the
stage hands call you, you're aware of that—Mona Chironi. I think
it's so interesting the parts that people cast themselves in for their
lives. And you have cast yourself as the cad. And you play it ever
so well. Such belief! A cad, of course, always believes he is chang-
ing the world. Hitler, after all, wanted to save the world from
socialism. I know—I know what you must play is Gregers Werle
in *The Wild Duck*. Lorenzo—I would produce that play to put
you in that role—a bumbling seeker of truth—that's you all over
and you play it so well.

[*Pause.* LORENZO *stares at him*]

LORENZO Geoffrey.
GEOFFREY Yes.

LORENZO I have just told you something important and tragic and earth-shaking and real. Will you react?

GEOFFREY No, I won't.

[*Pause*]

I mean I have.

[*Pause*]

I'm tired of this scene Lorenzo. I'm tired, it's late, tomorrow is the opening and if I were a member of the audience I'd be bored. [*to the audience*] You don't mind if we just end this scene do you?

[*Pause*]

[*to* LORENZO] I don't think they mind at all.

LORENZO Who are you talking to?

GEOFFREY People who paid good money to see this show. [*pause*] At any rate, everything changes after opening night. Oh, I almost forgot, I must cue in the next scene. I must say [*he speaks with* SYBIL's *intonation in the play*] "Marry her if you wish, it doesn't matter to me."

LORENZO Have you gone mad?

GEOFFREY No. [*melodramatically*] I've come to my senses I think!

LORENZO But—

GEOFFREY Lorenzo, [*stagily*] "Marry her if you wish, it doesn't matter to me!"

[*Lights begin to dim*]

Lights ... that's right. Wonderful. Right on cue.

[*Lights dim to black*]

ACT TWO, SCENE TWO

[*Lights up on* SYBIL *and* CECIL *on the deck*]

SYBIL Marry her if you wish, it doesn't matter to me, there are plenty of eligible bachelors out there with far more to offer than you, it's just that she's so tiresomely mystical.

CECIL Aren't you ever mystical?

SYBIL Only in the throes of passion—

CECIL What an odd expression: "the throes of passion"—

SYBIL Aptly named, because in true passion you throw absolutely everything away—

CECIL Have you ever done that, been so passionate that you've—

SYBIL Oh constantly, time after time, with each new love is a new passion, an inordinate extreme blinding passion, but no matter how hard I shake my arms or wave my fingers my diamonds don't seem to fall off.

CECIL So you have ... limited throes of passion?

SYBIL Limited only by my diamonds, yes—

[*The sound of the* MAJOR *chortling*]

Oh dear, will you entertain the Major? ... I'm afraid I've had all the chortling I can handle for one night ... Thanks ever so darling.

[SYBIL *disappears as the* MAJOR *enters*]

MAJOR Lovely night ... lovely night ... That's what I needed, some fresh air ...

CECIL It is a lovely night ...

MAJOR The stars, the sea breeze ... they always put things right—

CECIL That's not true for me ...

MAJOR [*irritated*] It isn't?

CECIL I've always been terrified of wide open spaces ...

MAJOR That's an irrational fear, my boy, there's no place for such feelings in a fine upstanding British lad like yourself.

CECIL Well if I'm so fine and upstanding, then why am I in love with her?

[*Pause. The* MAJOR *looks irritated, as if* CECIL *has been too familiar*]

I mean that is ... sir ...

MAJOR Yes, lad ...

CECIL Were you ever ... that is ... was there ever anyone, you see sir, I'm in quite a dilemma.

MAJOR Go on ...

CECIL Well I seem to be divided in two parts.

MAJOR I see.

CECIL There's a part of me ... I call it the British part of me, that says that I shouldn't marry Grazia because she is so strange and inexplicable and ... she disappears at the oddest moments, then there is what I call the American part of me which makes me feel that I must marry Grazia, no matter what happens, because I feel drawn to her, in a strange and mysterious manner, that is, Major—

MAJOR Yes, my boy—

CECIL Have you ever found yourself, that is, sir, acting un-British?

MAJOR What a question, dear me, how can I answer that one, how could I ever, how could anyone ever, well, that is, I suppose there was one time in India—

CECIL In India you felt un-British?

MAJOR Well never truly un-British. There was, however, in India, a young, oh well I don't know why I shouldn't tell you this, after all, this is a pleasure cruise isn't it, a young dancing girl named Liara who did the most marvellous acts with snakes, it really was quite ripping and—

CECIL And what ...?

MAJOR And well ... I remember she had lovely long arms, the arms of a young boy, which I thought at the time rather curious, and well, confound it, I made eyes at her. That's what happened. And that's

all that happened. Nothing really un-British about that—
CECIL It gives me hope, though—
MAJOR I'm glad to hear it, my lad.

[*He puts his arm around* CECIL]

CECIL Perhaps Grazia is my Liara.
MAJOR Perhaps ... my lad ...

[*He pats* CECIL*'s shoulder*]

Perhaps ...

[*They exit. Lights dim*]

ACT TWO, SCENE THREE

Lights up dimly. Laughter is heard. It is after opening night and very late. FAY *and* BRIDGET *are coming in the front door*

BRIDGET [*bitterly*] Everything changes after opening night ... that's right ... now I know I can't act, that's what ... I know I'll never do it ...

FAY Now darling that's not true at all. I'm sure no one noticed.

BRIDGET I noticed ... I noticed.

[*She is in the centre of the room now*]

Truth ... honesty! Real feelings ... bullshit, it's bullshit ... Who did they love tonight? Who did they really love?

FAY Well it's hard to say but—

BRIDGET Scrubby. They loved Scrubby. And I'm sorry but I don't consider that acting. I consider that ... caricature.

[*She sways around, drunkenly*]

FAY Be careful dear.

BRIDGET Why should I be careful? I'm tired of being careful.

FAY But you're a little drunk—

BRIDGET Yes ... I know ... You know—

FAY Come sit down here dear, it's safer ...

BRIDGET Oh alright ... and you know what ... you know who I think is really good and you know who I'm—oh I can't believe this—you know who I'm actually falling for? You won't laugh at me Fay?

FAY No, of course not.

BRIDGET Tom. Tommy. He's such a little charmer ...

FAY But Bridget you shouldn't ...

BRIDGET I know he's a fag but I don't care. When he tells me he wants me more than the sun and the moon I just want to rip off all my clothes and run away to Acapulco with him. The last thing I want to do is say my next line. [*she starts to cry*] Oh Fay ... I'll never be an actress. I've always wanted to be an actress but now I see ... it will never happen ... it's so sad ...

FAY There, there now dear, you can be anything you want to be.

BRIDGET No you can't. That's what grandmothers and mothers always tell you but you can only be what you are capable of being and if you try to be anything else you end up unhappy. I don't like acting. I don't like actors. They give me the creeps.

FAY [*hurt*] Do I give you the creeps?

BRIDGET No Fay no.

[*She leans up against* FAY]

You're wonderful.

FAY I think you're wonderful too.

[FAY *sits with her arms around* BRIDGET. *Slowly,* FAY *turns and gazes at the incoherent, bleary-eyed* BRIDGET. FAY *kisses her on the lips. The kiss turns more than just affectionate. Suddenly* BRIDGET *realizes what is happening and wrenches free.* BRIDGET *stands up*]

BRIDGET Hey— What's going on here—

FAY Nothing.

BRIDGET What do you think you're doing?

FAY Nothing. I was just trying to make you feel better.

BRIDGET But you were— Hey— Are you—

FAY Oh it's best not to go around putting labels on things. Why don't you just sit down and—

BRIDGET No, stay away from me. I can't believe you. I can't believe this house. I can't believe—

[*Laughter from outside the door*]

You people ...

[*She runs to the other side of the room, having a small coughing fit.* CELIA *and* LORENZO *enter with their arms around each other*]

CELIA Fuck off ... fuck off you scene-stealer.

[*She kisses* LORENZO]

LORENZO You're not so bad yourself—

[LORENZO *and* CELIA *kiss again*]

CELIA I can't believe, it you got more fucking laughs than I did with that little character role—

[GEOFFREY *enters with his arm around* TOM]

GEOFFREY But Lorenzo you were born to play villains and villains always steal the show—
TOM Scrubby isn't a villain.
GEOFFREY Yes, but he carries the nasty news, that makes him as good as one. Who would like a drink?
ALL [*except* BRIDGET] Me ... me me ...
GEOFFREY If Bridget will remove herself from the front of the liquor cabinet, then I will pour everyone a lovely—
BRIDGET Alright.

[*She moves away angrily*]

CELIA Well, well.

[*Awkward pause*]

FAY She had a bad night.
BRIDGET You stay away from me.
FAY [*hurt*] I'm sorry.
GEOFFREY Everyone please, I think we've had an incredibly successful

opening night, if I do say so myself, and we're obligated to toast. [*he opens a bottle of champagne, it spills*] Oh dear all over everything— To the company to the play ... Here everyone take a glass— Tommy help me—

TOM You've spilled everywhere—

GEOFFREY I'm a clumsy drunken old man—

TOM Yes I know—

GEOFFREY You're supposed to disagree with me. Here everyone—

[GEOFFREY *and* TOM *hand out glasses.* BRIDGET *won't take one*]

To us. To the company.

LORENZO To Lucius Quilby, the author!

[CELIA *runs up to* GEOFFREY]

CELIA To Geoffrey Gregson the most beautiful man alive I wish I had a dick so I could fuck him!

GEOFFREY [*laughing*] Alright then, to me. And to the theatre. Our only hope! Our only salvation!

FAY To the theatre!

LORENZO The theatre!

CELIA The theatre!

TOM The theatre!

BRIDGET You make me sick. All of you.

GEOFFREY What was that, my dear?

BRIDGET You make me throw up. All of you.

CELIA Oh darling ... are the drinkie poos going to your head?

BRIDGET Yes they are but it doesn't make things any different. It just makes me even more angry. Mr. Geoffrey Gregson I've decided to leave the acting profession as of tonight. I'll finish the run if you want me to but that's it for me as an actress.

GEOFFREY Ahhh, well, and the theatre will be much the worse for it. You showed great potential in this evening's—

BRIDGET Oh shut up. I don't want to show potential. I just want to be a person. A real person. With real feelings and goals. And you are a bunch of liars. I have never met so many liars at one time in my life. All of you ... you say one thing and you mean something

else, you're always flattering Geoffrey and none of you mean it and
if he says he likes the play then you like it if he says he hates it you
hate it, if he told you it was a lousy opening then you'd all decide
it was lousy and go home and cry there isn't a real feeling or
thought among the whole lot of you you're just a bunch of pup-
pets. You're all dead. You're all just as good as dead.

GEOFFREY Are you sure you aren't auditioning my dear, for the revival
of *Out to Sea*?

BRIDGET Oh fuck off. Can't a person ever be real around you? Does
everything have to be a performance?

GEOFFREY [*building to a booming theatrical voice*] Oh yes, my dear,
yes. Because all the world's a stage and since you're only here once
you might as well get a STANDING OVATION!

[*Pause*]

But I can see there's no point arguing. You're set upon playing the
role of righteous young thing and there's no stopping you now.
But darling, it's such a thankless part.

BRIDGET Oh!

[*She runs to the liquor cabinet and grabs the champagne bottle and
smashes it in the fireplace*]

That's what I think of your *theatre!*

[*She runs off. Pause. Everyone looks around uncomfortably*]

FAY Pardon me ... I must see if I can help her—

GEOFFREY Oh please do Fay, do.

CELIA Well that sure put a damper on the old fucking celebration.

LORENZO She wasn't very good really.

CELIA Where? On stage or just now?

LORENZO Both.

GEOFFREY I agree. She lacks ... vocal technique. Throwing the bottle
was a sort of a last resort for the rhetoric she couldn't muster.

CELIA Cheap special effects.

LORENZO Steven Spielberg at his worst.

GEOFFREY Yes.
[*Pause, uncomfortable again*]

CELIA [*fake yawn, looks at the men*] Well boys. I think it's time I put these weary old bones to bed.
GEOFFREY Goodnight Celia. You were charming.
CELIA I know. I just wish I had some of Lorenzo's laughs. More business. That's what I need. I'm so tired of playing with my train.
GEOFFREY Start eating it.
CELIA That's it, I'll eat my train. Eat my train—I love it! [*slight drunken hysterics*] Well goodnight.

[*Pause*]

LORENZO & TOM & GEOFFREY Goodnight.
CELIA Lorenzo. I said goodnight.
LORENZO So did I.
CELIA Lorenzo. Come on, you look pretty tired too now.
LORENZO I think I'll finish my champagne.
CELIA Lorenzo.
LORENZO Yes?
CELIA Look.

[*She walks over to* LORENZO]

[*to* TOM *and* GEOFFREY] Excuse us. [*in a stage whisper to* LORENZO] Can't you see they want to be alone?
LORENZO I'm perfectly aware of that.
CELIA [*quieter whisper*] Please Lorenzo, it's none of your—
GEOFFREY Perhaps we shouldn't be listening.
TOM I sort of feel like I'm eavesdropping.

[*She turns to them*]

CELIA We're going up to bed.
LORENZO Yes.
CELIA The only way I could get Lorenzo to go upstairs was to promise him that he could press his ugly hairy body against mine, fully

clothed mind you, for a moment or two outside of my bedroom door.

GEOFFREY A sacrifice of the highest order.

LORENZO But I'm allowed one warning.

GEOFFREY Ahhh ... go ahead.

LORENZO [*to* GEOFFREY] Watch out. We love you.

GEOFFREY Yes, that's lovely, now goodnight.

LORENZO [*a warning to* TOM] And goodnight to you.

CELIA Have fun guys.

[CELIA *and* LORENZO *go up the stairs, arguing. Pause*]

TOM What was that all about?

GEOFFREY Drama ... little internal dramas.

TOM Oh. I see—

GEOFFREY & TOM No you don't. [*they laugh*]

[*Pause*]

TOM So.

GEOFFREY So.

[*Pause*]

You have improved vastly.

TOM I have?

GEOFFREY Your playing. Especially in dress rehearsal, mind you—
Tonight you were big on nerves—

TOM Yes, I know—but tell me about dress rehearsal—

GEOFFREY Dress rehearsal you were lovely, really lovely. An ability to give oneself up to a role, and it is such a silly role, ingenue.

TOM It is silly yes—

GEOFFREY But it's the role you've been cast in—

TOM Not only here, but in your life as well?

GEOFFREY Pardon me?

TOM In the play, in the theatre which is your life I have been cast as the ingenue as well.

GEOFFREY How very audacious and perceptive.

[*Pause*]

Yes, of course you have.

[*Pause*]

It's not a thankless role you know. Though it may seem silly at first.

TOM I know it's not thankless at all.

GEOFFREY And you are considering playing it?

TOM Do you think I'm good enough?

GEOFFREY For some reason I feel you must have hidden wells of passion and emotion memory.

TOM For some reason, I think you're right.

GEOFFREY You'd have to get over the fact that I have reconciled myself to being the Major. "I am old, I am old, I shall wear the bottom of my trousers rolled."

TOM I find your wrinkles sort of ... charming.

GEOFFREY Well then there is potential for this becoming very ... very interesting.

TOM You won't think I'm sleeping with you just to get another part.

GEOFFREY Well the fact of the matter is you won't get another part by sleeping with me. Automatically.

TOM Ahhh.

GEOFFREY You'll have to audition like everybody else. That's a totally separate matter.

[*Pause*]

TOM I s— I won't say it.

[*Pause*]

GEOFFREY No don't.

[*Pause*]

There is one small thing, though. We should get this out of the

way, just so that all of the details are cleared up—
TOM I like to sleep on the left side of the bed, I don't find any sexual
positions offensive and I like teddy bears.
GEOFFREY Actual stuffed animals?
TOM Yes.
GEOFFREY How baroque.

[*Pause*]

No that was not the particular detail to which I was referring.
TOM No?
GEOFFREY No.

[*Pause*]

It's not really of any great consequence and I think I am less interested in the truth of your answer than in how you answer but the
question is this.
TOM Yes?
GEOFFREY Do you ... do you have ... that is, are you inflicted with
... that is ... *the* disease?

[*Pause*]

TOM *The* disease?
GEOFFREY Yes.
TOM Do you mean ... what I think you mean?
GEOFFREY I expect so.

[*Pause*]

TOM Ahhh oh yes. Lorenzo. Yes. That's what that was all about.

[*Pause*]

He has a big mouth hasn't he.
GEOFFREY He's cast himself as the cad, the truth-seeker in his own
dramas. I do hope he's porking Celia up there, though I know

TOM   As to how I got this disease. Well I have my theories. I think you
have to imagine a twelve-year-old boy wearing just a hint of make-
up standing around the washrooms at the Hudson's Bay Centre if
you really want to start thinking about why. That's where the disease started, I'm sure of it.

[*Pause*]

Do you want to hear more about my disease?
GEOFFREY   [*hypnotized*] Yes.
BRIDGET   I want to cry.
FAY   Well, go ahead dear.

[*She goes to* BRIDGET]

CELIA   Why?
BRIDGET   It's so unbearably sad that life is so short. Now for some rea-
son it seems so clear what I would have liked to do.
FAY   What?
BRIDGET   Everything I was afraid to—
FAY   Yes, fear seems quite silly now doesn't it, aboard this ship, this
ship of death.
TOM   It may be painful for both of us. My disease will torture you at
times as it will torture me. It is painful but sometimes it is also
very beautiful for it makes me conscious of my own mortality.
This disease, it repels; but in a strange way, it attracts. It bewitches, it alarms, it keeps us in suspense. Life is never dull, of that I
can assure you.
GEOFFREY   And what is this disease?
CELIA   I don't know about you ... but I suddenly feel ... dreadfully
happy.
FAY   A dreadful happiness.
CELIA   Well we're dead aren't we, but somehow we're still talking,
regretting, discussing, arguing, and in a minute or two, Scrubby
will bring our drinks.

[SCRUBBY *enters on cue*]

SCRUBBY Can I get you something mum?

TOM You know what it is, I won't use clinical terms with you. But I think if the truth be told, you who dislikes the truth so much, I think the truth is you have it too. Do you think so?

GEOFFREY Oh yes I do.

[*He moves over to* TOM]

Please, tell me what is your disease?

FAY I'll have a glass of sherry.

CELIA The same for me please.

BRIDGET Nothing for me.

TOM Dare I say the words? Dare I speak its name?

GEOFFREY But you must. You must.

SCRUBBY Whatever you say mum.

CELIA You won't have a little sherry? Now?

[*Pause*]

That is ... why put it off?

BRIDGET Perhaps I will ... live dangerously ... that is ... die dangerously ... perhaps I will ...

TOM My disease is ... my disease is—

[TOM *and* GEOFFREY *sit down on the couch.* GEOFFREY *leans towards* TOM. *They kiss*]

Love!

BRIDGET I found what I was looking for. Do you know why I didn't want to marry Cecil?

FAY Why no dear, no.

BRIDGET Because I think ... I was a little in love with death ...

CELIA I think those who are truly alive always are my dear, they always are.

TOM My disease is love. It's love!

[GEOFFREY *sinks into* TOM*'s arms*]

122

It's love!

SCRUBBY A sherry for you mum.

CELIA Thank you.

SCRUBBY And for you.

FAY Thank you Scrubby,

BRIDGET What about me?

SCRUBBY But you don't drink sherry mum.

BRIDGET I do now Scrubby, I do now.

SCRUBBY [*turning away*] Bleeding passengers on this bloody ship.
[*under his breath*] Can't make up their minds.

TOM Love!

SCRUBBY Them's human beings for you. Don't know whether they're coming or going. Wots a body to do! Wots a body to do!

[*All freeze: the three ladies with their drinks,* SCRUBBY *on his way out the door and* TOM *and* GEOFFREY *in each other's arms. Blackout*]

[*End*]

IN WHICH PIER PAOLO PASOLINI SEES HIS OWN DEATH IN THE FACE OF A BOY: A DEFACEMENT IN THE FORM OF A PLAY

In Which Pier Paolo Pasolini Sees His Own Death in the Face of a Boy: A Defacement in the Form of a Play was first produced by Buddies in Bad Times Theatre at Buddies in Bad Times Theatre, 142 George Street, Toronto, in June 1991, with the following cast:

PASOLINI Darren O'Donnell
BOY Shaun O'Mara

Director / Set Designer: Sky Gilbert
Lighting Designer / Stage Manager: Gwen Bartleman

Characters

PASOLINI, thirty (also plays GRACIOUS)
BOY, seventeen (also plays GOODNESS)

Time

1975.
Now.

Setting

In the original production the set consisted of two chairs. Many of the monologues and some of the scenes were performed in the audience. Certain scenes were played beside the audience near the exit doors of the theatre so that the audience could not hear or see everything. This lent a mysterious and surreptitious air to the proceedings.

Celia is much more particular about what goes into that particular orifice than she leads the world to believe.

[*Pause*]

Well?

TOM Can I have the rest of the champagne?

GEOFFREY Certainly.

TOM Music?

GEOFFREY You'll have to imagine it in your head. Celia broke the tape deck.

TOM Alright.

[*Music: theme from* Magnificent Obsession. *As* TOM *talks, the* Theatrelife *set gradually changes into the set for* Out to Sea]

When people ask me if I have the disease I never know quite what to say. There are different answers for different people because different people understand things so differently.

[CELIA, FAY *and* BRIDGET *enter in their period costumes for* Out to Sea *and the two plays*—Out to Sea *and* Theatrelife—*begin to happen at the same time*]

FAY [*gently*] I wish things could have gone differently.

CELIA I don't at all. I'm perfectly happy with the way they went.

BRIDGET But for me, you see, nothing really happened at all.

TOM So you see, how I explain my disease has a lot to do with who is listening. First I should tell you that I am not dying of it. Not yet. I may someday. I do not think that to die of it would be such an awful fate. I can think of worse things to die of. Maybe I will die of this disease, maybe you will. Maybe neither of us.

FAY So you have no regrets?

CELIA None whatsoever. I've always known what I wanted to do and then I've done it.

FAY I've always known what I wanted to do, but I rarely dared do it.

BRIDGET I've always wondered what to want, or if it was right to want anything.

Lights up on a bare stage. PASOLINI *enters from the same door that the audience uses. He walks intently over to an audience member and pulls up a chair and sits opposite him or her. He stares at the audience member*

PASOLINI   Should I? Moral question. I have met a questionable boy. A boy of questionable. Hah. Origin. Hah. Morals. Hah. He is questionable. What do you think? Do you think I should go with him? The first problem you see is that I am asking you. That is the bourgeois thing to do. You phone your friends. You ask advice. You phone a doctor a lawyer. The local priest. What do you think? What do you think I should do?

[A BOY *enters from any door that is to the side or rear of the audience. The sound of the door closing is heard. In the dark, he pulls up a chair and sits beside an audience member. He is less visible to the audience when he sits. He puts his feet up on a riser, relaxed]*

BOY   So he wants me. I know he wants me. Don't ask me *why* he wants me. I just know. So what do you think? You think I should go with him? Do you? I don't know. Sometimes I feel like it and sometimes I don't. He looks like he might have a big dick. What do you think? Do you think he has a big dick? Huh?

[Both PASOLINI *and the* BOY *launch into conversations with the audience simultaneously]*

PASOLINI   So you see in the mere asking of the question I see my own bourgeoisness reflected and it sickens me it makes me sick those who prevaricate those who lie those who would not act who would not live who would think first and act later those who would rather not commit themselves who would be somewhere

else than where it is happening you tell me how they can stay
home. Can I tell you know how he smells how the night smells
and what there is in the air the boys their pants are already wet
they are already soaking with pre-cum and you want me to stay
home you ask me to stay home or worse yet to ask some advice to
make a decision to think it out there are those things which one
cannot think about which lose their beauty as we speak as we discuss decide rationalize realize whimper whine rest worry wander
instruct weigh will write wonder. Well the time I spend deciding
whether or not my death is in this boy's eyes is time wasted if
death is there I will find it or it will certainly yes certainly find me.

BOY Sometimes you can tell about their dicks from their hands or
their noses well he looks pretty promising eh or sometimes that
doesn't work then it's disappointing or maybe he has something to
smoke or maybe he'll buy me a drink or maybe he has a big apartment with porn or maybe he doesn't. I don't know. I'm bored. I
haven't been laid in awhile but I'm not that horny. [*pause*] But
then again who knows maybe I can get something out of it.
[*pause*] It's going to be cold tonight I'd like a place to sleep so
maybe I can sleep with him he reminds me of my Dad you know
my Dad's like him dark and weaselly I bet he tells a good story
like my Dad and if he doesn't what'll I do? If he doesn't have a big
dick or tell a good story or have a big apartment or have porn or
drugs or something I'll just kill him I'll just kill him I'll just fucking kill him.

[*Blackout. Lights up on the* BOY *standing in the corner of the stage
smoking, chatting with his buddies*]

BOY Yeah well I let him have it. Yeah. I killed him.

[*Pause*]

Oh the guy was a fucking hairdresser right? He was a fucking hairdresser. I couldn't believe it. This guy it was so easy he liked to get
tied up and I knew that other people knew that he liked to get
tied up and so I figured if I tied him up and I cut his stupid little
fucking throat no one would give a fuck. And no one did.

[*Pause*]

Yeah there was this investigation but everybody said he was a stupid fucking hairdresser who liked to get tied up and when they heard about that it was no shit they just stopped investigating.

[*Pause*]

What can I say? He was a stupid fucking hairdresser. [*he does a fag imitation*] What can I say?

[*Blackout. Lights up on* PASOLINI *pacing around in the audience. He is very angry*]

PASOLINI And what I find is the most incredibly stupid question of all came from this little insipid intellectual friend of Laura's. Oh I don't know why she sees him the stupid little ...

[*Pause*]

Oh she invites these people over it's like a grab bag it's a party Laura is more *social* than I am she likes to be *social* though I can't imagine why—why be with people unless it's a sure thing and he makes some remark like "I've heard about you Pier Paolo what a contradiction in your nature that you this great artist this great intellect—" Suck this I felt like saying at that point. "You great—" Whatever he called me of the Italian whatever "and every night you go out on the streets looking for sex. Don't you find, Laura, that is a contradiction?" and I wanted to yell at him, That's the whole fucking point you idiot that is *not a contradiction* the *intellect* and *the sex and the night* are *the same thing what is the difference* the stupid fucking little—

[*Pause*]

He'll find out he has a dick in a few years then he'll be in deep trouble.

[*He exits. Lights down. Pause. Lights come up dimly on the stage. The* BOY *is to the side of the audience, smoking a cigarette. Pause.* PASOLINI *comes in a door that is to the side of the audience. The audience has to crane their heads to see. Nothing is heard except for laughter and mumbles. The* BOY *laughs as* PASOLINI *makes him offers.* PASOLINI *cajoles. They joke. Finally they go off together out the side door. Pause. Blackout. The* BOY *re-enters. It is pitch black. The* BOY *is drinking from a bottle* PASOLINI *has bought him.* PASOLINI *runs in*]

PASOLINI You see ... you see ... you see ... I told you—

BOY Wow ... what is this ...

PASOLINI This is a theatre—

BOY A movie theatre?

PASOLINI A theatre ... for plays.

BOY For plays ... Who comes to see them?

PASOLINI Nobody anymore. Nobody ever did. Who goes to see theatre anyways ...

BOY [*laughing*] Alcoholics ...

PASOLINI [*laughing too*] Yes, alcoholics, like you.

[*They kiss*]

Let me find a light—

BOY What do you need a light for?

PASOLINI So I can see you ... I like to see you—

BOY What do you want to see me for? ... I don't understand ...

PASOLINI Because I do ...

[*He starts up the stairs to the audience, holding onto chairs, tripping over audience members in the dark*]

Look, I paid for the wine ... I get to do anything I want to do ...

BOY For one bottle of wine? You're crazy ...

PASOLINI No I'm not crazy, but I'm not as drunk as you ... shit ... I'm tripping over seats ... do you know there are still seats in here? ... I'm tripping over seats— I know there's a light in here somewhere—

BOY So you've been here before—

PASOLINI Once or twice ...

BOY You mean I'm not the first?

PASOLINI Of course you're not the first. Why would you want to be the first? That's stupid and boring. Now, to be the two thousandth, that's really something—

[*He turns a light on in the theatre. The stage is illuminated*]

BOY Two thousand? You've done it with two thousand?

PASOLINI Last week I think. I might have lost count. There. Now I can see you.

BOY Those seats are really weird.

PASOLINI Yes, they are.

[*They both stare at the audience*]

BOY It's kind of like we have an audience.

PASOLINI Yes, well. I like that too.

[*He sits down in the audience*]

So ... here we are ...

BOY Here we are ...

PASOLINI Ah yes ... I like looking at you ...

BOY So what was the big deal? Why did you bring me here? I'm not going to suck you off you know. I don't do that.

PASOLINI I know that.

BOY So what's the big deal?

PASOLINI I've got a very special proposition for you.

BOY Hey well ... I'm all ears.

PASOLINI Good. So this is it. This is the deal. You come home with me. I have lots of wine. I have lots of pizza. You eat and drink as much as you want—

BOY You have drugs?

PASOLINI Not today.

BOY You have porn films?

PASOLINI Oh yes, I have lots of those—

Darren O'Donnell as **PASOLINI** and O'Mara as the **BOY** (top to bottom)

BOY With girls in them?

PASOLINI Yes, with girls in them—

BOY Yeah well I like the ones with girls in them.

PASOLINI Good for you. [*clearing his throat. His tone changes*] So you come home with me and you eat and drink as much as you like and you'll probably feel like farting that's okay you fart in my face I don't mind and you feel like taking a big shit well go right ahead. You don't have to go to the toilet if you don't want to. You can just take a dump right on me.

BOY [*he stops drinking, amazed*] What?

PASOLINI You heard me.

BOY Did you say that you—

PASOLINI I said you don't have to use the toilet. You can use me. That's all. So ... what do you say? Lots of food—all the food you want.

BOY [*laughing derisively*] I guess so. I guess you'll feed me that's for sure if that's what you're into.

PASOLINI Anything you want to eat. I've got it.

[*Pause.* PASOLINI *looks at the* BOY. *The* BOY *laughs*]

BOY You're kidding right?

PASOLINI Do I look like I'm making a joke?

BOY No. [*pause*] You're crazy.

PASOLINI That's right, I am.

[*Pause*]

BOY [*wavering*] Hey, look, you think I'd do something like that?

PASOLINI Yeah, sure, why not? You've got to use the toilet but instead you don't use the toilet. You use me.

BOY Fuck. Forget it man.

PASOLINI No?

BOY No.

PASOLINI Okay.

BOY Okay.

PASOLINI Okay. Guess we'd better go then.

BOY Sure. It's okay with me.

[PASOLINI *turns out the lights. The* BOY *starts laughing*]

Fuck I can't believe it ... I can't believe you ... I can't believe this whole thing ...

PASOLINI Yes, well, it's a very strange world we live in ...

BOY You're not kidding.

[PASOLINI *suddenly takes a hold of the* BOY *in the dark. A scuffle*]

Hey what are you—

PASOLINI [*in a strange voice*] You want to do it—

BOY What— Hey!

PASOLINI You want it ... I know you want it ... I always know when you guys want it—

BOY Hey you, let go of me ... you ...

[*They struggle in the dark. Lights come up suddenly on the* BOY *holding* PASOLINI *by the throat*]

HEY YOU FUCKING LET GO OF ME OR I'LL FUCKING KILL YOU DO YOU HEAR ME, I COULD FUCKING KILL YOU JUST LIKE THAT AND I'LL DO IT DON'T YOU WORRY!

[PASOLINI *stares at him. He is terrified. Blackout. Pause. Lights slowly come up on* PASOLINI. *He sits alone in a chair centre-stage, smoking*]

PASOLINI I am constantly astounded by the reverence with which these boys hold their assholes. And even more than that, their shit. One wonders, when one is in a bourgeois reflective mood, one tends to wonder what might happen if the sphincters of the world ever loosened up. Would it be diarrhea as so many fear or would it be instead the fine firmly packed feces of an adolescent: gleaming and immoral, proud and bursting with yesterday's lunch. I myself tend to believe it would be the latter. Certainly we fear the sphincter, that's hard to say, "fear the sphincter", and with good reason. Daddy smacked it when we were little and Mummy cried when it did its doodoo on the floor. There is an order must be an order no incest no rape no murder no deceit no stealing no homosexuality no coveting lusting wanting spewing stalking obsession desire beyond the point where it, sensibly, produces children. What would happen if these rules were to be broken? Some sort of pagan ritual I imagine. You see in a world such as this, a world which, understand me, is without any knowledge of its own real history because history goes back much further than D'Annunzio, it goes back further than Hitler Christ Alexander it goes back … well, I needn't tell you what it goes back to. You know. And that is what you're so afraid of. Don't you see? It's not your asshole, it's not your shit. It's all that stuff back there that says you're merely a human crouched on the ground gathering sticks making great giant farts that everybody can hear. So as you can see, I perform a public service. In a way. I help the boys, because their assholes are so *tight*, those boys, I help them to release their sphincters. It is up to me. It is my God-given mission.

I will tell you a story. It is a story of a very old homosexual I know who had been fucked in the bum so much that he no longer had any muscles back there. He was beginning to get a lapsed rectum which means the rectum begins to fall out of the sphincter. It was not a pretty sight. And you will not believe me if I tell you he was quite perverse, he used to catch little birds and feed them to his cat—for he loved that cat very much—and he would only partially kill the birds because he would not want the cat to lose out on its fun. As you can see he had quite lost his mind and certainly all sense of propriety. That is what happens when your asshole loosens up too much *you lose your mind.* Just thought you might like to know. Just thought you might be interested in the Eleventh Commandment: *do not under any circumstances loosen your sphincter.*

[*Pause*]

Just reminding you, Moses.

[*Blackout. Lights up on a bare stage.* PASOLINI *enters from the same door that the audience uses. The* BOY *enters from a side door. As before, they both choose an audience member, pull up a chair and sit down. They talk to the audience simultaneously*]

BOY Hey you're not going to believe this well I certainly didn't believe it I mean there are some real perverts in this world eh now let me tell you what this guy wanted me to do to him I'm not kidding right he takes me down to this old place this theatre but not before I got some wine out of him oh a nice bottle and he promised me more but shit [*laughing*] shit shit is right ... what he wanted. This guy I couldn't believe it this guy says to me, "So I'll feed you lots of pizza and you'll probably feel like farting and that's okay and you might even feel like taking a dump too"—I couldn't believe this guy was saying this to me but he was. So he says to me, "If you don't feel like using the toilet," he says—fuck I couldn't believe this—"If you don't feel like using the toilet you can just take a dump on me," well I couldn't fucking believe it man well what do you think [*pause*] are you kidding me? Do you think I'd stay there no way man no way I got the fuck out of there he was crazy man but could you believe it I couldn't fucking believe it.

PASOLINI It was a very interesting and quite amazing experience for the first time in my life I met my own death and he was a boy a very handsome boy I cannot describe his face to you but I saw it there and above all things that is what lured me perhaps he will kill me today, perhaps tomorrow perhaps never at all but the sight of my own death in his eyes was enough to give me an erection and it is not so much because I long for death. [*pause, thinking*] Not so much that. It is more as if— [*thinking harder*] Bear with me. It is as if, well, obviously coming to terms with an inevitable future face to face is that not what the innocents of the past understood oh to see them to be with them wandering underneath the trees and hiding behind the rocks what was there for the innocents to discover? Everything and that is what I long for a world where everything is discovered where the surprises have not been prescribed and sometimes I think that was the world that Jesus wanted a world where the surprises were real and the answers to questions not foretold make me wrong I want to be mistaken I want to undo all that has been done and go back to a very frightening place where there are no answers and, I fear, no microwave ovens.

[*Blackout. Pause. Shuffling around in the dark. Music:*

Cheery pre-show tune. Lights up on GOODNESS *and* GRA-
CIOUS. *They both have stylish kerchiefs around their necks
and they sit on chairs. They are eating chocolate cake*]

GRACIOUS Goodness!
GOODNESS Yes?
GRACIOUS I wasn't talking to you.
GOODNESS No?
GRACIOUS No. I was making an exclamation.
GOODNESS Well then, exclaim.
GRACIOUS Well, what I wanted to know is ... who made this
    cake?
GOODNESS Not I said the little chicken. [*he laughs*]
GRACIOUS Was it chicken?
GOODNESS I don't know.

[*They both laugh*]

It is good cake though, isn't it?
GRACIOUS Goodness it is, Goodness.

[*Pause*]

So I was thinking the other day.
GOODNESS Very good for your *brain* that *thinking*.
GRACIOUS Yes, I was thinking about a moral idea.
GOODNESS Oh my gracious can I handle this so soon after
    dinner?
GRACIOUS Well I hope so. This is important, now listen. This
    is a moral dilemma.
GOODNESS Alright I'm listening. I love trying to figure out
    moral questions. It reminds me of Sunday School.
GRACIOUS Didn't you just love Sunday School? It was so safe
    there. Like one big condom.
GOODNESS Anyway.
GRACIOUS Anyway. This is the moral dilemma, and I want
    you to figure out an answer.
GOODNESS Alright. I will. Don't worry. You know I'm very

good at this.

GRACIOUS I know. So this is the question: what should be done with those people who violate basic moral laws?

GOODNESS Oh that's very broad.

GRACIOUS Well—

GOODNESS Couldn't you make the question more specific? I find the question too broad. Too broad to even consider. For instance what moral law? To what specific moral law are we referring?

GRACIOUS Oh dear, do I have to come up with one?

GOODNESS Well I can't answer the question if you don't.

GRACIOUS Oh alright. Moral law ... alright I'll pick something that is so completely disgusting that you couldn't possible find it ... tenable. Let's say ... a person who likes to poop on people.

GOODNESS Oh *Gracious!* [*he puts down his cake*]

GRACIOUS What?

GOODNESS Please, *Gracious*, please. I'm eating.

GRACIOUS Well I know but you should be able to separate your—

GOODNESS But I can't ... that is just so disgusting, I just can't ... now I couldn't possibly swallow any more cake.

GRACIOUS Well you're getting too fat anyway.

GOODNESS *Gracious!*

GRACIOUS *Goodness!*

GOODNESS *Gracious!*

GRACIOUS *Goodness!*

GOODNESS What?

GRACIOUS What? [*pause*] Listen to my question will you?

GOODNESS Well, alright, but I certainly couldn't eat any more cake. And I don't quite understand how you can either. So. What's this *moral* question?

GRACIOUS Well let us just consider the case of person who enjoys defecating on other persons.

GOODNESS Oh dear. Well. Let's see ... then he ... I presume it is a he.

GRACIOUS Well it could be a she. Let's call it *it*. So *it* likes to go around pooping on people.

GOODNESS But I don't understand.

GRACIOUS What?

GOODNESS Why would anyone want to go around doing something like that?

GRACIOUS Well some people do.

GOODNESS How do you know?

GRACIOUS I just know. I read.

GOODNESS But I just can't imagine ... it's just so unimaginable. No one would ever do that ever.

GRACIOUS Well let's say they do.

GOODNESS But I don't understand.

GRACIOUS *Goodness.* How are we suppose to solve the moral argument if you find the question too disgusting? That's the whole point of moral questions, that you sometimes have to deal with disgusting things.

GOODNESS Oh well I suppose you're right.

GRACIOUS Of course I'm right. So here is a person who enjoys defecating on people.

GOODNESS Alright, I have a question.

GRACIOUS What?

GOODNESS Does it ask them first? Does it ask them if it can defecate, or does it just do it?

GRACIOUS I don't see what difference that makes.

GOODNESS Well of course it makes a big difference. It's a matter of consent. Consent makes all the difference under the law.

GRACIOUS Oh alright. [*he puts down his cake*] They always ask first.

GOODNESS They do?

GRACIOUS Yes.

GOODNESS They walk right up and say, "Can I defecate on you?" Something like that?

GRACIOUS Yes.

GOODNESS Oh well, let me see. I think ... [*pause*] I think that ... I think that they ... I think that they should be put to death.

GRACIOUS For pooping on people?

GOODNESS Yes.

GRACIOUS But why?

GOODNESS Because ... well I hope I don't need to tell you ...
I just find it morally repugnant ...

GRACIOUS But that's not a reason—

GOODNESS Certainly it is ... moral repugnance is something
everyone understands everyone has a sense of moral
repugnance. I think that moral repugnance is a very good
reason to—

GRACIOUS What if I told you I find you [*he grabs a fork and
suddenly turns savage*] *morally repugnant Goodness!*

GOODNESS What? Gracious, I—

GRACIOUS *Goodness I don't like your name I don't like your stu-
pidity all I want to do is to kill you, to kill you over and over
again so that there is blood all over everything.* [*he stabs*] *I
want you dead do you hear me Goodness oh God I hate your
name dead and stabbed and writhing* [*he stabs*] *and in
agony your guts spilling all over you tight-arsed little twit
from hell.* [*pause*] *There, I killed him.*

[*Suddenly* GOODNESS *rises up with a fork and stabs* GRACIOUS]

GOODNESS *No you don't Gracious!*

[GRACIOUS *dies. There is a pause.* GOODNESS *looks down at
the body. Pause.* GOODNESS *cries, theatrically*]

O my God what have I done ... what have I done ... O
Lord forgive me ... forgive me O God ... dear Lord ...

[*He stops crying. Pause. He stands up and looks at the audience*]

Well I just wanted to say that some of you may have
found the preceding dialogue and perhaps the activity disgusting. There may have been times when you even felt
the urge to leave the theatre. I think that's a natural
response considering the subject matter that was presented. But I'm glad you stayed through to the end because
... well, what I want to say is this: these are the author's
words but they also come from the bottom of my heart.

This play contains many nasty subjects.

[GRACIOUS *gets up*]

GRACIOUS And disgusting situations.

GOODNESS But we have all worked very hard on this production in the hopes that just one single person in the audience ... perhaps one child [*he breaks down in tears*] will hear what we're saying and turn away from ... I can't go on ... [*saying the other actor's real name*] Darren—

GRACIOUS That's okay Shaun, I'll take over with the message here— We can save one person, perhaps even one young person from a life of drugs or promiscuous sex, because what's really important, what we've discovered is most important about life is just plain old-fashioned warmth and affection. Not sex. Just love.

[*They put their arms around each other*]

GOODNESS & GRACIOUS *Love.*

[*They smile out at the audience. A burst of applause on tape. Lights slowly dim to black*]

[*As soon as the lights hit black* PASOLINI *and the* BOY *begin talking*]

BOY Hey— What are you—
PASOLINI You want to do it—
BOY What— Hey—
PASOLINI You want it ... I know you want it ... I always know when you guys want it ...
BOY Hey— Let go of me—

[*They struggle. Lights come up on them briefly.* PASOLINI *is terrified. He stares at the* BOY. *Blackout. Lights come up immediately. The actors are gone*]

[*End*]

143

MY NIGHT WITH TENNESSEE

My Night with Tennessee was first produced by Buddies in Bad Times Theatre at Buddies in Bad Times Theatre, 142 George Street, Toronto, in June 1992, with the following cast:

TENNESSEE WILLIAMS David Ramsden
JAMIE ANGELL Christofer Williamson
CRUMMY MULLIN Peter Lynch

Director / Set Designer: Sky Gilbert
Lighting Designer / Stage Manager: Gwen Bartleman
Lighting Technician: Fiona Jones

Characters

TENNESSEE WILLIAMS, sixty-five
JAMIE ANGELL, fifteen
CRUMMY MULLIN, twenty

Time

Summer 1979.

Setting

The set consists of the interior of **TENNESSEE WILLIAMS**'s hotel room in Vancouver, B.C. A large double bed and a cane-backed chair dominate the room. Clothes and newspapers are strewn everywhere. The café scene is created by placing two café tables and three chairs onto the stage.

Lights up on CRUMMY MULLIN *in bed. He is in his underwear. The bed is post-sex*

CRUMMY Oh yes you're asking me well. Well it was I remember well this great time I had with well it was the first great time actually I had with I remember I was about ten years old this was back in 1970 or something I don't remember when exactly and we had these cousins in New York City and we were just sort of the poor cousins—the poor *folk* from Toronto you know—the boring folk and there were these fascinating cousins Stephen and Melinda— very white names—in New York City that lived with my mother's half-sister, who she hated but that's neither here nor there and well for me at ten years old it was like a real opening up so to speak of my soul to the universe or something to the dark side to the underbelly I'll never forget driving in my cousins' car and Stephen was cute—freckles but cute—and playing "Dedicated to the One I Love" on the radio and back at home finding a copy of *Catcher in the Rye* and I asked my half-aunt about it and she said it was a book with a lot of dirty words in it so I read it and it changed my life and we got into a minor accident with Stephen's car where I was almost killed and I was supposed to lie on the insurance and then staying up all night playing Monopoly with Stephen and Melinda in Scarsdale. Melinda with the long blonde hair she was beautiful and dumb and nasty and I couldn't believe this that we were staying up all night and then I asked Stephen about this and they just said that that was what they did, you know? They were night people and they just stayed up all night and slept during the day and my mother said that was very strange and didn't approve but that to me was the most fascinating thing in the *world* you know staying up all night and sleeping all day and sure enough that's what happened to me I became this creature of the night this night person. I think that was my first association with this world that I live in now. So to speak. Poppers?

[CRUMMY *holds up a bottle. Lights dim on* CRUMMY. *Lights up on* JAMIE ANGELL *sitting at a café table*]

JAMIE [*embarrassed*] It's no big deal. I met Tennessee Williams and everything. Yeah. [*pause*] No. He's a really nice guy. [*pause*] No. Nothing happened. [*pause*] Well he did ask me to do this pretty weird thing. [*pause*] No it didn't have anything to do with sex. Get out of here. No. [*pause*] It was sort of more of a performance. Yeah. It was okay. [*pause*] I guess I've got something to tell my grandchildren. [*pause*] I know he's a fag and everything, but he's a pretty big writer, right?

[*Lights dim on* JAMIE. *Lights up on* TENNESSEE WILLIAMS *at his desk*]

TENNESSEE [*speaking with a marked Southern drawl*] In my house in Key West, I used to have this wonderful lighting effect. It was unlike any other lighting effect one could achieve in the world of theatre. The problem with it, of course, was that it was in the bathroom. I had a lovely skylight in the bathroom and in the morning the light would cascade from this skylight, it was a con-centrated beam a heavy concentration of light. And the beam would fall into the centre of the toilet, because Frank would always leave the lid up even when there were guests, I remember how Anna would yell at him, "*We don't all have penises thank you very much you know some of us have to sit down!*" Anyway, this very concentrated beam of light would fall or rather shoot every morn-ing into the very centre of the toilet and the toilet was a deep green porcelain and there was no other word for it it would look very lovely and poignant and it would make me want to cry. This toilet in the morning illuminated by this incredible sunlight would make me want to cry. The only thing was I felt very strange telling people about it. Getting all excited about my toilet. I could only tell certain people, in fact. Like Carson McCullers. It took a very special type of person to understand.
[*Blackout. Music: "Dedicated to the One I Love," The Mommas and*

The Poppas. Lights come up on JAMIE *at his table eating his breakfast.* CRUMMY *and* TENNESSEE *sit at a table in the middle of the audience.* CRUMMY *is talking as they read the paper*]

CRUMMY "Dear Abby. What shall I do? My husband doesn't care about me any more. He used to send me flowers and chocolates and take me out to dinner at the finest restaurants. Now he ignores me and watches TV. Is there another woman? How can I tell? Signed Perplexed in Peetawken. Dear Perplexed. Marriages go through stages. You can't have true romance every day of your life. It's time to work at keeping the relationship special. Bring him flowers. Wine him. Dine him. It might be up to you to put the spark back in your marriage." What do you think, Tenn?

TENNESSEE [*ignoring him*] Mmmm.

CRUMMY [*with a Southern accent*] Why I had the most amazing dream last night Tennessee. It was the French Revolution and people were begging us to punch holes in their nipples and all their guts were spilling out of them. What do you think of that?

TENNESSEE Mmmm.

CRUMMY I think I should dye my hair. Do you think I should dye my hair? Would you still love me as a blond?

TENNESSEE Mmmm.

CRUMMY Or maybe I should just cut my head off. What do you think of that? Then you could fuck my face whenever you wanted. Just take my head out of the closet and fuck it. How convenient. What do you think about that Tenn? *Hey Tenn!*

[*He grabs the paper that* TENNESSEE *is reading*]

TENNESSEE [*annoyed*] What?

CRUMMY I'm talking to you honey.

TENNESSEE I'm not listening. [*he straightens the paper*]

CRUMMY Do you think the romance has gone out of our relationship? You never stuff crumpets up my bum any more.

TENNESSEE There's no room for anything *more* up there.

CRUMMY I know. [*he shuffles around a bit*] Since we shoved the kitchen sink up there it's been a little crowded. Ahhh ... debauchery. [*pause*] Healthy muffin? It'll add inches to your dick.

TENNESSEE [*his head still in the paper*] Truman is dying.

CRUMMY Oh shit. Poor guy. But you don't care do you?

TENNESSEE No I don't care. I don't care at all. [*he puts down the paper and spills his rage*] He's a vicious vicious little man. I can't begin to tell you how he hurt me, how he hurt everybody—

CRUMMY Oh you have—

TENNESSEE Using his friends as cheap fodder. That's not art. It's not even reportage. It's sleaze. But I *hate* the fact that I'm gloating. I never thought I'd gloat at someone else's misfortune.

CRUMMY Oh, you do it all the time. When President Nixon—

TENNESSEE I mean *real* people. I don't mean *politicians*. [*pause*] Oh my God.

[*Music: a selection from* La Traviata. *Something—perhaps the light changes—makes* TENNESSEE *notice* JAMIE, *who is eating a muffin*]

Look.

CRUMMY Look where?

TENNESSEE There.

CRUMMY Where?

TENNESSEE There.

CRUMMY I don't know what you're looking at.

TENNESSEE Well I don't want to point.

CRUMMY Well what part of the—

TENNESSEE Over there ... by the balcony. Do you see that ... *vision.*

CRUMMY What that ... that *kid* eating a muffin?

TENNESSEE That's not a kid eating a muffin.

CRUMMY Oh, well then, who do you—

TENNESSEE I mean ... that vision in the sunlight. The amazing thing, over there.

CRUMMY Oh God.

TENNESSEE Oh God is right. Thank heaven for small mercies.

CRUMMY And he probably is.

TENNESSEE What?

CRUMMY Small.

TENNESSEE Don't be disgusting.

CRUMMY I'm being disgusting. *I'm* being disgusting? I can't believe this! You're the one who's being disgusting. Listen to me. Listen to me. [*he bangs the table*] *Listen!*

TENNESSEE Will you be quiet? People are staring—

CRUMMY I don't care if people are staring. You're not doing it again.

TENNESSEE [*still staring*] What?

CRUMMY You know what.

TENNESSEE I don't know what.

CRUMMY Yes you do.

TENNESSEE [*turning to him*] Crummy. Don't take that tone with me.

CRUMMY I'll take any tone I want to. Listen. [*he bangs the table again*] *Listen!*

[TENNESSEE *looks at* CRUMMY]

I'm not putting up with you turning some perfectly normal human being into an angel again. I'm just not putting up with it.

TENNESSEE Oh please—

CRUMMY No, I won't "please" anything. I know what happens when you talk like that. When you get that look in your eye.

TENNESSEE Look. He's cutting the crusts off his toast.

CRUMMY Well let's call Walter Cronkite, see if we can get in on the evening news, who cares if he's …

TENNESSEE Those crusts are just too … hard for his tender insides—

CRUMMY His tender insides— That's it I'm leaving—

TENNESSEE Look at him now—

CRUMMY [*standing up*] Goodbye. I'm going to Wreck Beach.

TENNESSEE [*absently staring off*] Have a good time.

CRUMMY [*staring at* TENNESSEE] And I'm going to get laid in the bushes. I'm going to get stoned and laid in the bushes because I'm tired of this shit Tennessee. It's not cute any more. It's stupid and boring …

TENNESSEE Look … he's got a moustache … the milk made a moustache!

CRUMMY [*screaming*] *Ahhh!*

[*He runs out of the restaurant*]

TENNESSEE Now he'll have to wipe it off. He is wiping it off. How sweet. A boy like that can't go around with a moustache. He is a vision. I must know. I must find out if he's real. Is it possible? Could he be real? Do angels exist? This is an important metaphysical study. Yes, it most certainly is.

[TENNESSEE *wipes his face with a napkin and straightens his shirt. He stands up and carefully walks towards the* BOY *who is beginning to butter his muffin.* TENNESSEE *stands for a few moments away from the table just watching him. The* BOY *finishes buttering his muffin and starts to eat it. After a moment he notices that* TENNESSEE *is watching him. He looks up from his muffin.* TENNESSEE *steps forward*]

TENNESSEE I'm sorry.

JAMIE Wha— [*he looks behind him*]

TENNESSEE I'm sorry. I'm staring.

JAMIE Oh. [*pause*] At what?

TENNESSEE At you.

JAMIE Oh. [*pause, then confused*] What is it?

TENNESSEE You had ... a milk moustache on your face a minute ago.

JAMIE Yeah. I know. Didn't I wipe it off?

TENNESSEE Oh, yes, you did. There's no moustache any more.

JAMIE [*strangely*] Good.

TENNESSEE It wouldn't be right for a boy like you to have a moustache.

JAMIE Yeah, well, [*pause*] I can't grow one yet anyway.

TENNESSEE [*fondly*] I didn't think so.

JAMIE Sometimes I don't know if I'll ever be able to grow one. That would be a drag, eh?

TENNESSEE Oh ... I don't know. [*pause*] I'm sorry. Let me introduce myself. I'm ... Tennessee.

JAMIE Williams?

TENNESSEE Yes.

JAMIE Really?

TENNESSEE [*shyly*] You've heard of me.

JAMIE Yeah, well, we read you in school.

TENNESSEE I see. [*pause*] Are you here on a school trip?

JAMIE No. My Mom and I just moved here, we don't have a place to live yet. She has a job as a maître d'. And she tells fortunes.

TENNESSEE Oh. I'd love to have my fortune told.

JAMIE Maybe she can do it for you.
TENNESSEE I'd like that.

[*Uncomfortable pause*]

Listen.
JAMIE Yeah?
TENNESSEE I was wondering if ... if, well, you'd like to come and visit me.
JAMIE Visit you?
TENNESSEE Yes.
JAMIE Where?
TENNESSEE Well ... in my room.
JAMIE In your room?

[*Pause*]

Well that would be okay, sure. Only thing is ... I'd have to ask my Mom.
TENNESSEE [*fondly*] Ahhh.
JAMIE Yeah. But usually she says yes to things. If I beg.
TENNESSEE Then do beg her, why don't you?

[*He hands* JAMIE *his card*]

We'll expect you about eight o'clock.
JAMIE Sounds okay.
TENNESSEE Oh yes, one more thing. What do you drink?
JAMIE Alcohol?
TENNESSEE Well, that is—
JAMIE Well ... like I'm only fifteen. I'm not old enough yet. I don't really like the taste of it. Have you got any iced tea?
TENNESSEE Iced tea. Yes certainly. Most certainly. We'll make you a bucket. See you later young man.

[TENNESSEE *is leaving.* JAMIE *gets up; he is almost bowing*]

JAMIE Nice to meet you, Mr. Williams.

TENNESSEE Nice to meet you.

[*He stops*]

Oh. I presume you would like sugar in your tea?
JAMIE Yeah. And lemon, if it's not too much trouble.
TENNESSEE No ... no it's not too much trouble. Goodbye young
man. Young ... young man.
JAMIE Goodbye.

[TENNESSEE *exits, staring at* JAMIE. JAMIE *stands looking after him, then he sits*]

Wow. [*he takes a bite of the muffin*] Wait 'til I tell Mom.

[*Lights dim on* JAMIE. *Lights up on* CRUMMY *in a messy bed. He is on the phone and eating candy*]

CRUMMY But like I'm getting really pissed off. Even if he is Tennessee
Williams. I mean he doesn't even turn me on that much. You
know the first time I had sex with him you know what I had to
do, don't you? I had to keep saying to myself over and over I'm
really having sex with Tennessee Williams I'm really having sex
with Tennessee Williams. It was the only way I could get an
orgasm. [*pause*] No. I don't do that any more. Now I use the Arab
slave-boy fantasy. You know tied face down to a bed and force-
fucked by *Amal* with the thirteen-inch cock. It always makes me
come. [*pause*] Well ... no. I mean he doesn't have a very good
body. And he's *old*. But he's a good kisser. [*pause*] Because I like
him he keeps me entertained nobody I ever met talks like him.
[*pause*] Oh his cock is nice. Anyway, so there we are in the café
having this fabulous lunch and he sees this stupid kid and starts to
go all nuts. I could just *kill* him. [*pause*] Well we have an open
relationship and everything but in front of me? I mean I'm sorry
girl you may be Tennessee Williams but I won't put up with that.
Besides when was the last time you had a fucking hit? [*pause, he
giggles*] No he hasn't had a hit in *years*. It drives him *crazy*. If I really
want to upset him all I have to do is mention—

ROB ALLEN

Peter Lynch as CRUMMY

[*The door opens.* TENNESSEE *walks in.* CRUMMY *changes tack*]

Yeah, sure. If we're going to make it down to Wreck before sun-
down we'd better leave *soon.* Bring lots of money. I want to get
some acid. Okay. See you later doll, bye. [*he hangs up. Pause*] That
was Bob.

TENNESSEE Oh. [*he lights a cigarette*] How's Bob?

CRUMMY She's *hysterical.* Met some hooker with a huge wang and
almost bled to death last night.

TENNESSEE How nice for her.

[*Pause*]

CRUMMY So how was that retarded ugly kid you were trying to pick
up in the café. Was he as boring and straight as he looked?

TENNESSEE He was, in fact, a very nice boy.

CRUMMY That I find hard to believe.

TENNESSEE Crummy.

CRUMMY What?

TENNESSEE I hope you are not going to be difficult about this.

CRUMMY About what?

TENNESSEE Well, I've—

CRUMMY You didn't.

TENNESSEE Well, yes, in fact—

CRUMMY You didn't invite him over here for a threesome. You didn't.

TENNESSEE Yes I did—

CRUMMY Oh God fuck shit piss how many times do I have to tell you
that it takes *three* to make a *threesome.* I don't *want* to have sex
with him. I think he's *creepy!*

TENNESSEE Well if you don't want to then I certainly will have no
trouble—

CRUMMY I'm sure you won't. I hate it.

[*He gets up in a rage*]

I hate it when you do this it really makes me mad, it really does—

TENNESSEE What?

CRUMMY Run after these stupid kids it's so stupid and insulting—

TENNESSEE Insulting to who?

CRUMMY To yourself. Not me I don't care about me and obviously you don't either—

TENNESSEE Crummy. We have an *arrangement*—

CRUMMY Yes and I want the arrangement more than you. I need outside fucks just as much as you need them but having outside fucks is one thing I do it quietly in the bushes but you—you just get so embarrassing—

TENNESSEE Embarrassing to you. Wonderful for me.

CRUMMY So what if I said—

[*He gets a suitcase*]

What if I said I wasn't going to put up with it any more—

TENNESSEE Crummy please—I love you—

CRUMMY I love you too. But why don't you just get a little ... self-esteem. It's about time for it don't you think?

TENNESSEE What, if you don't mind telling me, do you mean by *that?*

CRUMMY I mean elderly playwrights should have a little more self-respect than to go *gaga* over fourteen-year-old boys.

TENNESSEE He's fifteen.

CRUMMY How do you know?

TENNESSEE I asked him. And I am not, as of yet, elderly.

[*Pause*]

Have you finished?

CRUMMY Yes and I'm leaving. And I don't know when I'm coming back.

TENNESSEE Do you mind if I say something first?

CRUMMY If it's going to be your I-have-an-infinite-capacity-for-beauty speech you can forget it. I've heard it before. What could you possibly have in common with—

TENNESSEE Nothing. Don't you see? That's the point.

CRUMMY Oh, I see, if only I was dumber. If only I hadn't heard of Tennessee Williams—

TENNESSEE He's heard of Tennessee Williams. It's not that.

CRUMMY Then what is it, because I'd like to know. I'd really like to know. I'm cute. I'm a good cocksucker. I'm a lot of fun. What's the fucking problem?

TENNESSEE There is no problem. Unless you want to make it. I want to see his legs. I want to see his ass. I want to see where they meet. I want to see his belly. I want to see the hairs that go from his belly to his cock. I want to see his cock. His balls. Is there a lot of hair there? Is there hair on his legs? What are his nipples like? Is it all baby fat under those clothes or is it lean and muscled? I want to know. I *have* to know.

CRUMMY So ... you're going to sniff poppers and watch him take off his clothes.

TENNESSEE Perhaps. I wish you wouldn't put it so crudely—

CRUMMY Well if you can't hack the truth—

TENNESSEE I'm sorry, Crummy, but this is uncalled for. This whole little scene is uncalled for. You know the rules. You know the arrangement. And I'm sorry you're going to hear the beauty speech again—

CRUMMY No I'm—

[TENNESSEE *grabs him*]

TENNESSEE Listen. I have an insatiable craving for beauty. It keeps me alive. I must participate in that beauty. I cannot just let it walk by. I must love it, talk to it, caress it. That is the way I am made. It is my fuel. It is what keeps me going. Your beauty and the beauty of others. I'm a beauty junkie. I will not give it up. No matter how many lectures I get from sexless straight couples and uptight little queers like you. And if that's the way I'm going to die, with the poppers in my nose and some young butt revealed before my face, redolent, plump, hairy, smelly, smooth, white, tanned, pliant, hard, muscled, young, brown, black, yellow, red, green then yes that's the way I want to go. You knew that about me when we started. If you insist on suggesting that I have no self-respect then you had better go somewhere else for your love and companionship. I have respect for who I am and what I do. If you don't, that is your problem, not mine.

[*Pause*]

CRUMMY Or maybe—if you'd had a single good review, in the last ten years—you wouldn't even give beauty the time of day.

TENNESSEE [*enraged*] *Get out of here!*

CRUMMY Tenn listen—

TENNESSEE *Get out you little whore and don't come back do you hear me don't you ever come back!*

CRUMMY Look, I'm sorry—

TENNESSEE *Sorry's not good enough—*

[*He pushes* CRUMMY *out the door*]

Get away from me.

[TENNESSEE *bangs the door shut.* CRUMMY *bangs on it from the other side*]

CRUMMY *Tenn! Tenn!*

TENNESSEE [*quietly to himself*] Perhaps it doesn't occur to you, young man, that Fifteen-Year-Old Beauty cannot hurt me. And I am—

[*He lights a cigarette and sits on the bed*]

I am very easily hurt.

CRUMMY *Tenn! Tenn! I'm sorry!*

TENNESSEE [*to* CRUMMY] *Fuck off!* [*to himself*] I await the angel ...

[*Lights dim. Music: a selection from* La Traviata. *Lights come up. It is night and* TENNESSEE *has been drinking heavily and doing poppers. He is passed out in the rumpled bed in his underwear. Suddenly his bottle of rye falls out of his hands and onto the floor with a thump. He wakes up and peers out from under the covers*]

Is it the angel? Is it the angel that has come for me? I am ready for the angel. And when the angel comes he will not hurt me because he does not know how to hurt one as me, one as wounded as me. Yes, you can kiss them. My wounds. Yes, you can hold me. Yes you can tell me that I've done a very good job living and it's more than alright that it didn't work out as I expected. Yes, angel. I am ready to hear all that. I am ready to go to a place where I will not be hurt any more. That's what heaven is, isn't it? Beautiful boys, with beautiful bodies only ... they don't hurt you. I have been thinking about my angel for such a long time. I knew an angel once ... but ... he went away. Is that you? My angel? Is it?

[*A knock on the door*]

Well that's either Crummy or the angel.

[*Another knock*]

Who is it?

JAMIE [*from behind the door*] It's Jamie, Mr. Williams. You asked me to come up today.

TENNESSEE Ah ... it is the angel ... the angel that was foretold in the prophecies. Yes ... the angel is here ... send in the angel—

JAMIE [*behind the door*] Do you want me to come back at another time?

TENNESSEE No ... no. *Come in! The door's open!*

[*Pause.* JAMIE *opens the door tentatively and comes in. He stands there in the moonlight in his T-shirt and shorts*]

JAMIE Hi.

TENNESSEE Why hello there.

JAMIE Did I come at a bad time?

TENNESSEE No ... you came at the perfect moment ... the most perfect moment of all.

[*He picks up the bottle of rye and holds it out*]

Would you like some?

JAMIE No ... like I said, I don't drink ...

TENNESSEE Oh you wanted some iced tea how stupid of me ... I fell asleep here, as is my wont, at times, in a drunken, that is, a relaxed creative sort of ... and well how do I express that is, I well, I ... I forgot.

JAMIE That's okay. I don't need any.

TENNESSEE I'm so sorry. Oh I feel terrible ... forgetting your iced tea, it was iced tea you wanted, wasn't it? With sugar and lemon.
JAMIE Don't worry. I'll be fine.

[*Pause*]

TENNESSEE Well sit down won't you ... and make yourself comfortable.
JAMIE Okay.

[*He sits on a chair, tentatively*]

TENNESSEE So your mother allowed you this outing?
JAMIE Oh yeah. She didn't mind. She thinks you're a great artist.
TENNESSEE Well that's very nice of her.
JAMIE She said that she read in the cards that I was going to meet somebody famous. And that was you.
TENNESSEE Your mother sounds like a grand and gracious lady. Is she from the South?
JAMIE No. She's from Brantford, Ontario.
TENNESSEE Well she sounds like a beautiful and genteel woman nevertheless. "Nevertheless" is a beautiful word, isn't it?
JAMIE Yeah.
TENNESSEE Well my young ... Jamie ... what is your last name, I never asked you your last name—
JAMIE Angell.
TENNESSEE Angel?
JAMIE Angell. With two *L*s.

[*Pause*]

I kind of get kidded about my name a lot at school.
TENNESSEE I can't believe it.
JAMIE That my name is Angell? It used to be Agnelli but my grandfather changed it.
TENNESSEE Ahhh. [*pause*] Well ... Jamie ... I think that's just lovely [*he takes a swig*] and I think that you're a very lovely boy.
JAMIE [*carefully watching him*] Thank you.
TENNESSEE Has anyone ever told you that you are extraordinarily

handsome for a boy of your tender years?

JAMIE [*pause*] Yeah.

TENNESSEE And what do you say when the compliments are proffered?

JAMIE I say thanks.

TENNESSEE That is very gracious. You should always acknowledge compliments. It is the very least that a well brought up young man can do. And I can see that you have been very well brought up. I suppose your mother loves you very much.

JAMIE Yeah.

TENNESSEE And your father?

JAMIE Oh, he's not around.

TENNESSEE Neither was mine. I think, Jamie Angell, that we are alike in many ways. You are intelligent. I am intelligent. Your schoolmates tease you. My schoolmates teased me. Your father has disappeared. So did mine. The only way in which we are not alike is in our appearance. I am old and haggard and ugly and you are a handsome boy in the very prime of your youth.

JAMIE I don't think you're ugly.

TENNESSEE That's very, very tactful of you to say so, but the truth is that I am falling apart.

JAMIE You don't look like it.

TENNESSEE Well thank you.

[*Pause. He takes a swig*]

Jamie.

JAMIE Yes?

TENNESSEE Could you do me an enormous favour?

JAMIE Sure.

TENNESSEE Could you take off all of your clothes, except for your underwear?

JAMIE Ummm. [*pause*]

TENNESSEE Yes, young man?

JAMIE Ummm. [*pause*] Why?

TENNESSEE I will be honest with you. I will be honest with you as I hope that you will be honest with me. I think you are extremely beautiful. I would like very much to see what you look like with your clothes off.

JAMIE Oh.

TENNESSEE Of course, if you'd rather not, I understand.

JAMIE I can keep my underwear on?

TENNESSEE Why most certainly.

JAMIE Well. I guess there wouldn't be anything bad about doing that. The only thing is these underwear have got a hole in them. In the back.

TENNESSEE Well I think we can overlook the hole ... so to speak.

JAMIE Okay. Should I ...?

TENNESSEE There's no time like the present.

JAMIE Right here?

TENNESSEE Most certainly. And take your time.

[JAMIE *begins to undress, with one eye on* TENNESSEE. TENNESSEE *takes a swig every now and then and watches* JAMIE. *It takes* JAMIE *a few minutes. When he is done he stands in front of* TENNESSEE. *Pause*]

JAMIE How's that?

TENNESSEE That is quite, quite lovely. You are nothing like I imagined you at all.

JAMIE No.

TENNESSEE It is always a surprise, always a veritable surprise, what someone has underneath their clothes. Now I would like you to do me one more favour.

JAMIE What?

TENNESSEE I would like ... first of all to tell you that you have a very nice body ... no nice is an awful word ... let's not say nice, let's say voluptuous, for a boy, voluptuous and tender and luscious and ripe and very, very tantalizing.

JAMIE I'm getting embarrassed ... [*he smiles*]

TENNESSEE Well and it's only right that you be embarrassed. You wouldn't be a boy at all if you didn't get embarrassed. You'd be a dinosaur. And you'd be extinct. Thank God you are not a dinosaur. Thank God you are a boy. The second favour I would like you to do for me is take this book—

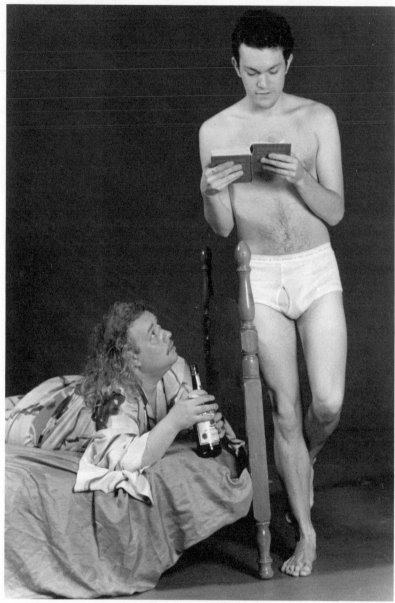

David Ramsden as TENNESSEE and Christofer Williamson as JAMIE (left to right)

[TENNESSEE *throws a small book to him. The book drops at* JAMIE'S *feet*]

—and turn to page seventy-six.

JAMIE Seventy-six.

TENNESSEE Yes, that is correct. And when you get to that page, I
would like you to read for me what is on that page.

JAMIE Okay. I found it. Ready?

TENNESSEE Yes, I think I am quite prepared. Let me just—

[*He adjusts a light on* JAMIE *so it is perfect*]

There ... that's better.

JAMIE [*reading to* TENNESSEE]
The Hill
by Rupert Brooke.
Breathless, we flung us on the windy hill,
Laughed in the sun, and kissed the lovely grass.
You said, "Through glory and ecstasy we pass;
Wind, sun, and earth remain, the birds sing still,
When we are old, are old ..." "And when we die
All's over that is ours; and life burns on
Through other lovers, other lips," said I,
—"Heart of my heart, our heaven is now, is won!"
"We are Earth's best, that learnt her lesson here.
Life is our cry. We have kept the faith!" we said;
"We shall go down with unreluctant tread
Rose-crowned into the darkness!" ... Proud we were,
And laughed, that had such brave true things to say.
—And then you suddenly cried, and turned away.

[*For a moment they both stare at each other.* JAMIE *holds the book
and* TENNESSEE *watches. Then* TENNESSEE *starts to cry.* TENNESSEE
reaches for the Kleenex]

TENNESSEE You will forgive me ... that poem always makes me cry ...
because Rupert Brooke is such a damned awful poet ... and I,
therefore, feel a strange affinity for his work ...

[JAMIE *comes over and sits on the bed*]

JAMIE Are you okay?

TENNESSEE Yes, I am okay ... as okay as I will be ... I suppose ever ... because you are here, it's just that ... you remind me very much of someone ... someone who left me a long time ago and he was a very kind person ... and you know how unfair it is when a very kind person gets ill and dies and you, as I say, remind me of him. That's all. It is a stupid and predictable reaction from a queer old man like me. Perhaps you should go now.

JAMIE Do you want me to?

TENNESSEE Well I don't want you to. What I want you to do is just curl up here in bed with me, but I have a feeling that you don't want to do that and I understand. I'm old and smelly and drunk and now crying and you should go. The short answer is yes, I want you to go.

JAMIE [*pause*] You're a really nice guy.

TENNESSEE Why thank you. And you're a gracious and charming young man. But I think you should put your clothes back on.

JAMIE Okay.

[*He gets up and starts putting on his clothes*]

I don't see why you say he's such a bad poet. I liked that poem.

TENNESSEE Well I like it too, but it is, if I may, so—so unreservedly sentimental, and art should not be that way, if it can possibly be avoided. But sometimes it is, and we cry about silly things we can't change. That was what happened to me.

JAMIE Are you sure you're okay?

TENNESSEE Of course, I'm okay. I'm just not drunk enough yet to go to sleep. I have a friend who should come by—

JAMIE The one from the café?

TENNESSEE Yes oh that is maybe he won't we quarrelled today I'm afraid I was very nasty with him as he was with me—

JAMIE Because I can stay and read more poetry. I don't mind reading in my underwear, really I don't. It was kind of fun.

TENNESSEE No. It's quite alright. I shall be better by myself ... I start getting maudlin now ... this is merely the beginning, young man, merely the beginning …

JAMIE Well thanks for asking me up. I had a good time. I can tell my grandchildren I met you.

TENNESSEE Yes you can … but please don't tell them what happened.

JAMIE Yeah, I promise.

[*He starts to go, then pauses at the door*]

Well it was wonderful meeting you. Thanks again.

TENNESSEE You're very welcome. Thank you.

JAMIE Well, goodbye.

TENNESSEE Goodbye, Frank.

JAMIE What was that?

TENNESSEE Oh … nothing.

[JAMIE *walks out awkwardly and closes the door.* TENNESSEE *curls up in bed. Music: "Dedicated to the One I Love," The Mommas and The Poppas.—the climax of the song The lighting changes.* CRUMMY *enters the room with his bag*]

CRUMMY Tenn? Tenn?

TENNESSEE [*waking up, suddenly*] What?

CRUMMY Tenn. I'm back. I'm sorry. I know you told me never to come back. I'm sorry. That was a really shitty thing to say. I didn't mean to say it. Do you forgive me? Are you okay? I shouldn't say things like that. [*suddenly rushing his words*] I just got jealous I guess which is stupid I know we have an arrangement I just get weird insecure I don't know. Sorry. I hope you forgive me because I miss you already and I don't want to fight, really I don't.

[TENNESSEE *is crying again*]

What's the matter? Was that kid here? Was it okay?

TENNESSEE Yes. It was okay.

CRUMMY Did you fuck him?

TENNESSEE [*blowing his nose*] No. I had him read me some poetry. He just … reminded me very much of Frank.

CRUMMY Oh, yeah. Frank. Well maybe that's the problem. Maybe that's the trouble with us. I mean I really respect what you had with Frank and everything but I mean I know I'm not Frank I'm not beautiful and kind and perfect on the outside and on the inside I'm just Crummy Mullins and you know how I got that name because I'm crummy.

TENNESSEE I know. Come here.

[CRUMMY *goes to* TENNESSEE]

Please get into bed now. And I'll tell you something about Frank.

[CRUMMY *climbs into the bed*]

You see ... what I divined some time ago, is that, in fact, I always have been looking for Frank, and even when I was with Frank I was looking for Frank, because you see, Frank wasn't even Frank.

CRUMMY I don't get it.

TENNESSEE Frank is an idea. An idea of something that can never be gotten a hold of. So when you find that [*he sniffles*] I'm looking for Frank, or thinking about him or searching the eyes of boys for Frank, just remember nobody is Frank, and not even Frank was Frank. Do you understand?

CRUMMY Not really.

TENNESSEE Well you just curl up with me and be my angel then ...

[CRUMMY *curls up. They lie entwined in the bed, in the moonlight. Pause*]

CRUMMY Tenn?

TENNESSEE Yes.

CRUMMY Did you do poppers?

TENNESSEE With poetry. No we most certainly did not.

[*Pause*]

CRUMMY Tenn?

TENNESSEE Yes.

CRUMMY What's the point of searching for something that you'll never

ever in your whole life get?

[*Pause*]

TENNESSEE A very deep question.

[*Pause*]

CRUMMY So what's the answer?
TENNESSEE That's what heaven is all about. Heaven is where the angels are and boys don't hurt you. Let's go to sleep and dream of heaven.
CRUMMY But what if there isn't a heaven?
TENNESSEE Shhh. Be quiet boy ... and dream ...

[*They curl up together. Music: "In paradisum," Requiem, Fauré*]

[*End*]

HESTER: AN INTRODUCTION

Hester: An Introduction was first produced by Buddies in Bad Times Theatre at Buddies in Bad Times Theatre, 142 George Street, Toronto, in May 1994, with the following cast:

HESTER Christopher Peterson
MAN Daniel MacIvor

Director: Sky Gilbert
Designer: Andy Parks
Lighting Designer / Stage Manager: Gwen Bartleman
Sound Technician: Fiona Jones

Characters

HESTER, a drag queen of indeterminate age
MAN, the proverbial heel

Time

Now.

Setting

Hester: An Introduction is a performance melodrama in the original sense of music / drama. The set is very simple. A forbidding door is the main set-piece. A kitchen table, a chair and a magazine rack are centre-stage. On top of the table are magazines, chocolates, an ashtray and all of the other accoutrements of a drag queen. In the original production there was a red carpet leading to the doorway highlighting HESTER's many treks to the door.

The man playing HESTER should be adept at mime and lip-synch; he can use these talents to best effect when supported by the music, which always plays until HESTER opens the door.

Pre-show music: "It Had To Be You," Betty Hutton.

Lights up. HESTER—*a beautiful, tragic and funny drag queen—is sitting at a table, smoking and drinking coffee. Melodramatic music: Delius. A knock at the door.*

HESTER Oh, I wonder who that could be.
She turns to the audience
Would you excuse me, for a moment?
She walks over to the door and opens it. She stares out in abject terror.
Oh my God.
A gunshot. She falls down dead. Blackout.

Lights up. HESTER *is smoking and drinking. This time she is also reading the paper. Melodramatic music: Delius. A knock at the door.*
Oh fuck.
To the audience.
Should I answer it?
Pause. She looks down.
I want to ... but should I? I don't know what to do.
Another knock, this time more insistent. She stands up, resolute.
I must answer the door, I have no choice.
She walks over to the door and opens it.
Oh hello I ...
Suddenly schoolgirlish.
I didn't think you'd come. But you have ... of course. Won't you come in? No ... well then stay outside then ... whatever you wish.
Pause.
No ... that is ... no don't please don't ...
She falls to her knees.
Don't I can't bear it if you ... no ...
She is hanging onto someone outside the door.
No ...please no ... please ... I can't stand it any more I can't ...

177

The person outside the door leaves. She cries. Lights dim to black.

Lights up. HESTER *is smoking and singing and humming and tapping her foot. Music: nervous jazz. Pause. A knock at the door. She ignores it. Another knock at the door. She mumbles to herself, incomprehensibly. Another knock. She gets up, goes to the door and very slowly opens it, looking down. She finally looks up, slowly. When her head is fully erect she lets out a bloodcurdling scream and slams the door. Blackout.*

Lights up. HESTER *is asleep in the chair. Music: Piano Intro to "More Than You Know," Blossom Dearie. A knock at the door. She wakes up with a start. She sips some coffee, hung over. Another knock. She staggers up, taking her cigarette with her, and opens the door. She leans over, smiles confidentially, and chats with whoever is there, laughing now and then until the lights dim to black.*

Lights up. HESTER *is bent over the table. Melodramatic music: Delius. A knock at the door. She lifts her head up.*
No. It can't be. Not again.
Another knock.
I'm not going to answer it.
Another knock.
Maybe if I don't answer it, he'll go away.
A pounding on the door.
Maybe not. Alright.
She walks to the door and opens it. She melts into and kisses whoever is there. She shuts the door, her back against it, and leans there, satisfied. She wipes her lips. She wanders away in a sexual haze. The door opens. A gunshot. She falls to the ground. Blackout.

Lights up. HESTER *is reading a book, eating chocolate with greedy delicacy. Music: bouncy jazz piano. A knock at the door. She ignores it, making a dismissive noise, shaking her head.*
Nanananana.
Another knock.
Nonononono.
Another knock.
Oh, alright ...

She goes and gets up, still engrossed in the book, walks to the door and manages to open it with one hand. She looks up casually.
Oh hi. Uh huh.
She is very interested, leans against the door and listens and responds.
Oh yes. Uh yes ... really, you don't mean ... not ... yes? Why that's oh ... excuse me.
She pops a chocolate it into her mouth.
Why I can't ... that's just so ... yes ... why I just never ... oh my God ...
She laughs wildly
Oh ... I don't believe it ...
She laughs wildly again
Really!
She laughs loudly as lights dim to black.

Lights up. HESTER *is sitting with her arms folded and her foot shaking nervously. She is waiting for something. A knock.*
What would happen if I just didn't ... if I just didn't open it at all?
Another knock.
What would happen? I mean, after all, it's up to me. I have will, I have volition. I have a life.
Another knock.
I just won't answer it. We'll see. There. We'll see now what happens.
The door bursts open. Organ Concerto music: Poulenc. A MAN *in a trench coat and hat enters. He picks* HESTER *up and carries her off like Fay Wray. She screams wildly as she is carried out the door. Blackout.*

Lights up. HESTER *is dusting madly and carelessly. She is trying to ignore the door. Music: 1950's TV-theme music. A knock at the door. She reacts in fear.*
Ahhh.
She tries to dust again. Another knock. Another fearful reaction, as if she has been struck.
 Ahhh.
More dusting, another knock.
Ahhh.

She braces herself. She walks to the door, steeling herself for the worst. She opens the door. A gorgeous light shines through the doorway. Music: "Exultate Deo," Poulenc. She falls to her knees, crossing herself, head bowed. The music plays to its end. Blackout.

Lights up. HESTER *is not in good shape. She is popping pills, pacing, drinking, smoking—the whole bit. Music: from* Dark Victory, *suggesting insanity and discordance. A knock at the door. She drops her pill bottle onto the floor.*

Oh fuck.

She picks up the pills and takes one more. She takes a swig of booze. Another knock.

Alright. I'm going to answer you. Whatever is there. I can take it. I've been through this before. Many times. It's not so bad. I'm strong.

She starts towards the door, then goes back to the table, takes another pill and a swig.

There. You dish it out, I can take it. I guarantee it.

She strides over, a bit shaky, and opens the door. A hand comes in and gives her a cute stuffed gorilla. She can't believe it.

Oh thank you. Oh— Isn't he— Oh, thank you so much ... thank you ... that's just so ... how can I ever ...

The hand slams the door shut.

It's a nice ... stuffed gorilla.

She stands holding it, a little sadly. Lights dim to black.

Lights up. The room is empty. Music: theme from Now, Voyager. *A knock at the door.* HESTER *enters with a bottle of liquor in hand and her hair wild. She is in a frenzy. She stands on the other side of the room staring at the door. Another knock. She pretends to be relaxed.*

Just a minute!

She puts down the bottle and takes out a compact. She tries to rearrange her hair and make herself up. Another knock.

I'll be there in a sec!

She is finally satisfied with herself and goes to the door. She opens it mid-knock. Pause. She smiles, prettily. Whoever is there spits on her. Pause. She slowly closes the door. She starts to wipe off her face. Blackout.

Lights up. HESTER *is pacing back and forth theatrically, wringing her hands, looking at the door. A knock. She stands perfectly still for a moment. Then she resumes her theatrics. Another knock. She is still. Then she resumes her theatrics. Another knock. She is still. The door opens. A* MAN *in a trench coat enters. He is also wearing sunglasses and a fedora.*

HESTER No please no, I'm sorry.

He moves towards her.

Look, I apologize.

He stops. Then starts again.

Please don't—

He gets close to her, then walks downstage towards a microphone. She stares at him, confused. He walks over to the microphone and adjusts it to his height. He taps the microphone and speaks into it.

MAN Hello, hello ... testing. Is this thing working?

Someone turns the microphone on.

There. So. What can I say. I just got back. I didn't have a very good time. The fucking car busted and I ... well I won't make excuses. It's not. It's not ...

His voice changes, becoming much less naturalistic, more formal. He speaks into the microphone.

Possible for me to be what you want.

He taps the microphone, a nice guy again.

Hey, is this thing working? So anyway, it just didn't come through. It just didn't happen and well, there I was wondering, thinking what the fuck am I going to do with myself, you know, and just got waylaid I guess. My usual, shit ... I will.

His voice changes again to a formal, deeper tone.

I will be everything you want except a couple of things which are very important to you. Those things will be missing.

He taps the microphone, his voice is back to normal.

Whew, that was a close one. Got a little bit too stoned there. A little bit too much. Too close to that proverbial edge, the proverbial edge we all hear talk about. Sorry about that. Geez. Well, where was I? Did I tell you ... did I happen to mention how swell you look? *Real* swell, really swell, yes. Better than ever. When you—

He stops and his voice changes again.

When you really need me, I'll call, but I'll be dead, in Vancouver.

How do you like ... how do you like—
A normal voice.
That is just not true. No. I would never. Must have been a mistake
or something. A little problem there. Something went wrong. Not
my fault. Don't you understand that?
A formal, deeper voice.
It's not my fault.
A normal voice.
Just so you know ...
Embarrassed.
I'm not ... very good at this ... sorry ...

HESTER *is still standing upstage. She has listened to this speech sadly,
bemused, and gives the audience a humiliated smile. Lights dim to
black. Music: "Sextet," Poulenc.*

End.

MORE DIVINE: A PERFORMANCE FOR ROLAND BARTHES

More Divine: A Performance for Roland Barthes was first produced by Buddies in Bad Times Theatre, 12 Alexander Street, Toronto, in October 1994, with the following cast:

ROLAND BARTHES Randall Lanthier
MICHEL FOUCAULT Mark Christmann
OLIVIER Mark Lonergan
GERARD / DAISY / HOOKER D. Garnet Harding
AMIDOU / BUTLER Christopher Sawchyn
YAWEH / JACQUES Jason Cadieux
MUSTAFA Bruno Miguel
PARISIAN / MOROCCAN BOYS Mario Moreira, Cameron D. Severin

Director: Sky Gilbert
Assistant Director: Franco Boni
Set Designer: Steve Lucas
Costume Designer: Wendy White
Lighting Designer: Bonnie Beecher
Music: Richard Feren and Dominic Giovinazzo
Stage Manager: Debbie Read
Production Stage Manager: Gwen Bartleman
Lighting Operator: Ruthe Whiston

Characters

ROLAND BARTHES, a philosopher
MICHEL FOUCAULT, a friend
OLIVIER, a student
GERARD (also plays DAISY EVERSO, HOOKER)
AMIDOU (also plays BUTLER)
YAWEH (also plays JACQUES)
MUSTAFA
2 cruising Parisian BOYS
2 playful Moroccan BOYS

Time

1980.

Setting

Paris. The set consists of five box-like structures. The homes of
MICHEL, ROLAND and OLIVIER are represented by three of these
boxes. The audience sits in another box. The fifth box, when
revealed, is a proscenium stage. ROLAND's home contains a tele-
phone and a chair and an oversized book—Chateaubriand's
Napoleon. OLIVIER's home has a child's desk and chair and rows of
books painted on the walls. In MICHEL's home, the walls are cov-
ered with S&M equipment. Each box, including the audience's,
has graffiti scrawled on the walls—the type of graffiti one finds in
washrooms. Each box has glory holes.
Morocco. Open space, very bright light. The contrast with the
Paris set, particularly in terms of lighting, should be as strong as
possible.

"I therefore have decked myself out in finery so that I might be in the company of a fine young man."
   —Socrates

Pre-show music: "I Love Paris," from the origival Cole Porter live
Broadway album of Can Can
Paris. A drizzly night, dark, dank and depressing. Lights fade to black
Lights come up, dimly. Music: a tape loop of the opening chords of
"Dialogues des Carmelites," Poulenc. What follows is a kind of ballet.
Schoolboys rush around in the rain, carrying their books and occasion-
ally stopping to cruise each other and perhaps to push a hand or
another body part through a glory hole. MICHEL FOUCAULT, ROLAND
BARTHES *and* OLIVIER *enter their homes, carrying their books, but*
not without cruising some of the boys along the way. When each is
finally ensconced in his separate box—and after a certain amount of
cruising has occurred through the holes in the walls—one of the boys
goes down on MICHEL. *Lights fade to isolate* ROLAND's *home. The*
boys begin to disappear. Perhaps one boy remains smoking somewhere,
perhaps he is waiting for OLIVIER *to leave*

ROLAND   I am amused, as I become older, to find myself reading
   Chateaubriand. Perhaps I am not amused. Perhaps I am saddened
   by it. Nevertheless, I rarely have the energy to do anything but go
   to sleep. Is this what it is all about, what it was all for? In ascribing
   to my existence a meaning, and in reading Chateaubriand, I find
   that my expectations of myself are perhaps as bourgeois as one
   would expect from one who has railed against the established
   order for his entire life. And will Olivier call? [*he stares at the*
   phone] I saw a boy at the Café de Flore this afternoon. He wore
   his grace like a young horse, his fingers were dirty, the bright red
   shirt was crowned with a tie. An affectation. Where did he come
   from? Where will he go? He was reading a fashion magazine. [*he*
   stares at the phone] And will Olivier call? He stares at the phone.

187

When I become conscious that I am reading out loud my own
stage directions I am seized by conflicting impulses. The first
impulse is to walk out of the play. Perhaps I should. Perhaps therein lies my freedom.

[*A couple of* BOYS *have gathered around* ROLAND'*s door. They are
cruising each other.* ROLAND *opens his door. The* BOYS *immediately
disappear.* ROLAND *closes the door*]

And then again, perhaps not. My second impulse is to act the
expected sad old faggot: it's to cry or something. Come now, you
expect it of me. And then I feel ... [*he tries to cry*] I feel ... that I
shall not do it well enough, and you, being the bourgeois audience
you are, you will demand your money's worth. Huge tears. Huge
bulbous tears, staining my costume. Perhaps also, you will demand
I smile through them, the tears. Perhaps also you will demand
more of me. So much that at the last moment I will feel I cannot
give it, but then, at the climactic point, I will.

[*Pause*]

Perhaps you will feel that there should have been a more elaborate
set. He looks at the phone. [*looks at phone*] The phone rings. The
phone rings. I thought I'd try that. Stating as a stage direction
"The phone rings". In that phone somewhere is Olivier. His strangled voice. His strangled lack of love for me. Oh, it's all so pitifully
predictable, I think I shall have a cognac and some chocolate,
which will upset my stomach.

[*The phone rings*]

Ahhh. It is Olivier. I will pause, so as not to appear too eager.

[*The phone rings again*]

To wait for the third ring is not brave, merely reckless, for young
men are impatient.

[*The phone rings again*]

The fourth ring—

[*He cannot wait.* ROLAND *grabs the phone. Lights up on* OLIVIER, *in his box, on the other end of the line. As* OLIVIER *talks on the phone a* BOY *is cruising him through a glory hole. During this conversation, various other* BOYS *cruise each other. Now and then, they pant and sigh, mirroring* ROLAND'*s discomfort with* OLIVIER'*s plans for the evening*]

Hello?

OLIVIER Roland.

ROLAND Yes?

OLIVIER Roland I just realized that if I were to abbreviate your name, charmingly and affectionately, it would be Role.

ROLAND Ahhh, yes. But you don't.

OLIVIER You wouldn't like that?

ROLAND I would have no feelings about it.

[*Pause*]

OLIVIER So, Roland darling, I have news.

ROLAND And what would that be? [*he lights a cigarette*]

OLIVIER I am taking Michel's course this year.

[*Pause.* ROLAND *holds the phone to his chest and sighs. The cruising* BOYS *all pant three times.* ROLAND *finally speaks into the phone, covering up his feelings*]

ROLAND Ahhh. Good idea.

OLIVIER You think so?

ROLAND Of course. He is a brilliant man.

OLIVIER People say he is very sick.

ROLAND Oh yes, in many ways.

OLIVIER People say this may be his last year to teach.

ROLAND It may very well be.

[*Pause*]

OLIVIER Does it bother you that I am taking Michel's course?

[*Pause*]

ROLAND [*very bothered*] Why should it bother me?
OLIVIER Because you and he diverge—
ROLAND In the realm of the political where I enter it, it seems to me
    that the individual's own imagination is efficacious. Michel would
    disagree on paper. In person, I am not certain—
OLIVIER Should I tell him that?
ROLAND You may tell him anything you like.
OLIVIER Why are you so cranky?

[*Pause*]

ROLAND I'm depressed.

[*Pause*]

Are you still interested ... in the play this evening?
OLIVIER Oh, yes, of course, what shall we go see?

[*He spies a* BOY *peering at him through a glory hole*]

Excuse me.

[*He drops the phone and goes over to the hole. The* BOY *runs away.*
ROLAND *speaks to the audience. Between each of his phrases, the cruising* BOYS *and* OLIVIER *pant, once*]

ROLAND I wait ... I smoke ... I wait ... I blow smoke rings ... I
    burn inside ... I—
OLIVIER Hello, Roland? Who were you talking to?
ROLAND No one. Who was at the door?
OLIVIER No one.

[*Pause*]

So, what shall we see? The Pinter or that revival of Dumas?
ROLAND I shall find the Pinter excruciating—
OLIVIER But everyone is talking about it—
ROLAND Hence my contempt. It will be endless. The Dumas will be
over quickly and there will be time for a coffee.
OLIVIER Whatever you say. I'll meet you there at a quarter to eight.
ROLAND Yes. [*carefully*] Yes, my darling. [*he smokes*]

[*Pause*]

Goodbye.
OLIVIER Oh Roland.
ROLAND Yes?
OLIVIER Do you mind, I've invited Michel?

[*The cruising* BOYS *expel three pants, mirroring* ROLAND's *pain.*
ROLAND *covers his feelings*]

ROLAND Ahhh. When did you do that?
OLIVIER I met him today, when I was signing up for his class.
ROLAND Ahhh, yes, well, why not?
OLIVIER Will you call him then?
ROLAND Why yes of course.
OLIVIER You don't mind?
ROLAND Of course not.

[*Pause*]

See you there.

[*They both hang up the phone. Pause*]

Ughghghghgh.

[*Now, after each sentence* ROLAND *speaks, the cruising boys moan,
mirroring* ROLAND's *pain*]

Why try? *Why try deliberately to hurt me? Why? Or am I trying deliberately to be hurt? Why? Why could I not say, "I am disgusted that you are taking this course with him"? Why? I called him "Darling". Ughghghghgh.*

[ROLAND *starts to cry. Then he squelches his emotions and picks up the phone. Lights up on* MICHEL. MICHEL *is having sex with someone through a glory hole in his apartment. The cruising* BOYS *are having sex as well. The set vibrates with the rhythm of fellatio*]

MICHEL Hello?

ROLAND Michel.

MICHEL Oh hello, Roland.

ROLAND Did I call you at a bad time?

MICHEL Why no, not at all.

ROLAND Listen, my young friend Olivier suggested you might come with us to the theatre this evening.

MICHEL Olivier?

ROLAND He is ... the one you ... called arrogant.

MICHEL Oh yes. The boy who wants to be you.

ROLAND Yes. [*he grimaces, cursing to himself*] That's the one.

[MICHEL *moans*]

What was that?

MICHEL Nothing. So what shall it be, I hope not the Pinter. He's so excruciatingly Anglo. The love that dares to pause too much.

ROLAND No, and it won't be over until late, and we'll miss the Café at its peak.

MICHEL What then? [*he moans*] Oh.

ROLAND What?

MICHEL Nothing.

ROLAND Michel?

MICHEL Yes.

ROLAND What are you doing?

MICHEL Trying. Oh. To fit into a very tight pair of pants. Oh.

ROLAND Ahhh. [*he grimaces*] So we'll see you at the Dumas at a quarter to eight.

MICHEL I'll be there.
ROLAND Goodbye.

[*He hangs up the phone. Pause. Lights dim on* MICHEL *and the cruis-ing* BOYS *who are all having orgasms*]

I'm certain he was having sex ... my God ... why does that bother me ...?

[*Lights fade on* ROLAND, *pacing and smoking. Music: "Prelude to Act Two, Scene Three," Dialogues des Carmelites, Poulenc.* MICHEL, OLIVIER *and* ROLAND *leave their homes, button their coats, pull out their umbrellas and walk towards the audience. The fifth box is revealed: a curtained proscenium stage. The three men meet in front of the audience, greet each other and sit in seats that are reserved for them in the audience.* OLIVIER *must decide who to sit with. He decides to sit with* MICHEL, *much to* ROLAND's *dismay. Before the play, rude boys hand out programmes to the audience for the play enti-tled "The Whore Is in the Closet Coughing: A Semiotic Melodrama". The prelude ends*]

[*Music: Offenbach. The curtains open on the proscenium. The sets are garish, made out of cardboard, with several clos-ets for people to hide in. The period is late nineteenth centu-ry. As in Victorien Sardou's "well-made play", sublimely evil villains and a secure moral order pervades. Lights up on* DAISY EVERSO, *a fashion editor, played by a boy in drag.* DAISY *is answering her mail, pen in hand*]

DAISY "Dear Daisy: My hips are too large and my breasts are too small, what should I do? Signed Fat and Flat-chested in Ferron." Well, let me see, I would say my darling, do not go out of the house, but because of fashion, you have every chance of re-creating yourself.

[*The phone rings. She answers*]

Hello? Yes, I would like two tickets to the Canary Islands

... for next weekend, yes, for my lover and myself, yes, a young businessman, decent, impeccable, but at the same time rakish and unpredictable. And the next weekend for Tahiti, for I hear the climate is mild there. Thank you. Goodbye.

[She hangs up and begins writing again]

Dear Fat and Flat: I think a blazer will do the trick. A blazer for the tomboy in you. I see you as something of an Anglophile, smitten with Proust, who loves to spend her weekends at the shore. Make sure the stripes are vertical.

[The phone rings. She answers]

My favourites? Why, Pascal and cool jazz, Heidegger and hip hop, the St. Thomas of Aquinas and Aqua Velva. Why yes, eclectic is my middle name. Yes, I shall be at the ball, it's after the hunt is it not? I'll be there for cocktails. Yes, after visiting the farm. At the château. Yes, thank you, goodbye.

[She hangs up]

Oh, the Countess Nun de Thierry can be such a bore. Well.

[She signs the letter she has been writing and puts it in an envelope]

These are ready for my messenger.

[The BUTLER *enters. He is evil]*

BUTLER Miss Daisy Everso?
DAISY Why yes.
BUTLER I am merely reminding you that the messenger will be here any minute.

DAVID HAWE

D. Garnet Harding as DAISY, Christopher Sawchyn as BUTLER and Jason Cadieux as JACQUES (left to right)

DAISY Of that I am aware. Oh how shall I dress today?

BUTLER Well, how do you feel?

DAISY Why, I feel smitten and smacking, deloused and déclassé, I have a tooth missing for so long I've been kissing and killing—I'm gay. Unbeknownst and bewary, demented and caring, I'm as cool as the wind and as hot as a thigh, no one could be as merry as I, or as sad. Quicken the pace of the lad, hairy with knickers, I'll take a kicker of champagne and Derrida. Frustrated and calm, I've been known to embalm, my emotions quite deep in a freezer. But what should I wear, I don't really care, oops, darling please get me a tweezer.

BUTLER Will you be wearing the South of France, then?

DAISY I think so, Max. And I shall have a snippet of sassy boredom for my ears, and a coquettish but discriminating ingenue on my feet and a naughty easygoing balanced carefree classic for my hands and my eyes ...

BUTLER Expecting company?

[*Music: a snippet of Offenbach.* JACQUES *pokes his head out of a closet, briefly.* DAISY *and the* BUTLER *don't see him*]

DAISY Before cocktails, I suspect I will be demure and determined, tender and tough, casual and cunning. My lover, the messenger, will soon be here, or my name's not Daisy!

[*The* BUTLER *opens a closet door and gestures for* DAISY *to enter*]

BUTLER Your closet?
DAISY Only momentarily and for the sake of fashion.

[*She disappears into the closet, but not without a theatrical stage cough*]

BUTLER [*chuckling in a campy and effeminate manner*] I am evil. In case you had not noticed. I am dressed in black.

[*Suddenly he steps downstage, out of the play. He appears more masculine. He whispers to the audience*]

And if that is not enough, I am forced by this postmodern director to cackle and wince and indicate at every moment that my motives are less than presentable.

[*He jumps up onstage again and resumes his effeminate overplaying of the role*]

But what is the cause of my evil [*he turns a bit into the Wicked Witch of the West*] Hahahahaha and your little dog too! Is evil merely a matter of a laugh and a moustache? No, it cannot be explained and what is further tragic for Daisy is that she lives in a world of weekends and cottages and ski chalets and mascara. She claims to be sassy and serious. But deep down she is a man.

[*Suddenly he leaps out of character again, walks downstage and speaks*

196

to the audience. He is, again, very masculine]

And since this play exists in some strange unimaginable moral order where homosexuality is the norm, God forbid, [*he whispers conspiratorially*] *I am a heterosexual actor.* Is there any way I can indicate this to you? Show you?

[*He sits down beside* OLIVIER *and chats with him, casually*]

True, I am playing a homosexual, but it must be possible for you, somehow, to understand that I am doing this [*becoming angry*] stupid campy drag queen of a director a favour by appearing in this godforsaken drivel. [*calming down*] I am liberal, I am open-minded. I am masculine and caring, sensitive and strong. If I appear homosexual to you it is only because I am so comfortable in my heterosexuality that you mistake me for being a gay. Also, I am a marvellous actor. But how does one indicate that one is a marvellous actor *and* a heterosexual stretching to fit a role which is alien to him—but to which he is sensitive—and still get good notices? Watch me.

[*He stands and goes back onstage and resumes his effeminate role-playing*]

> The letter. Daisy is a man, in case you hadn't noticed. I am evil, and like Iago, no amount of motive-seeking will deliver the answer why. I will switch letters with a signed confession in which Daisy reveals she is a man. Daisy's messenger, her lover, will read this letter, for he reads all of Daisy's mail. This will precipitate the tragedy. That done, I will now clean the closet.
>
> [*He opens a closet door, exits and shuts the door behind him.* JACQUES *enters heroicly*]

JACQUES I am Jacques and there is no finding me, I am quick and clever and handsome as the sea. [*he spies the letter*] Ahhh, Daisy's "male". As usual, I will read it unbeknownst to my charming mistress who is conceited and demure, dimwitted, lively and delovey and ... [*he reads*] a *man!* Oh how can that be? I have made love to her for over ten years, off and on. And now to discover she has all this time been a male! Let me explain this to you, for those of you who don't understand.

[DAISY *comes out of her closet and overhears him*]

How could I fuck a woman for ten years and not know she was a man?

[ROLAND *seems to have fallen asleep.* JACQUES *kicks his seat and he wakes up with a start*]

First of all, she sucked me off most of the time. Second of all, unless I was drunk, I avoided her cunt and if it was late at night, or very early in the morn, well, as the sailor says, any port in a storm.

DAISY Is that all you can say?

JACQUES What?

DAISY Any port in a storm? What about the Canary Islands?

JACQUES It's cancelled.

DAISY And Tahiti?

JACQUES I can't vacation with you! You're a drag queen. An invitation to ridicule ... I never loved you. It was all a lie. Besides ... [*to the audience*] What he's doing makes fun of women. It's also living in a fantasy which makes me a co-dependent, and ignoring his biological—

DAISY Oh shut up!

[*She shoves him in the closet*]

Get into the closet where you belong. That's it ... my lover knows the truth: I'm ... a man. All along I've been ... nothing more, or less ... I'm alone now. [*her line is a music cue, but nothing happens. She speaks louder*] I'M ALONE NOW.

[*Music: "Violin Sonata Movement Two," Grieg. Lights dim.* DAISY *speaks directly to* ROLAND *who is fascinated by her*]

I have reached the depths of despair ... I want to cry ... I know I can cry ... I want to give you your money's worth ... feel what it's like to be someone totally alone, someone who is living a totally pitiful life, a life without hope, a lonely life ... a life where there is only cognac, chocolate and Chateaubriand's *Napoleon* ...

ROLAND [*from the audience*] Wait a minute ... what did she say ...
OLIVIER Shhh.

[*A knock at the door*]

DAISY A knock at the door.

[DAISY *opens the door.* MICHEL *stands there. He is wearing a dapper wig and top hat*]

Why Gilles LaFleur, my alter ego and intelligent witty friend, and to whom I am sexually attracted now and then in a casual way, what are you doing here?
MICHEL I thought I might drop by and see if perhaps someone had discovered that you are a man.
DAISY Why they did.
MICHEL Jacques?
DAISY It was, in fact.
MICHEL —hates you.
DAISY I've locked him in the closet.
MICHEL Where he belongs.
DAISY Don't say that.
MICHEL I must. It's the truth.
DAISY What will become of me?
MICHEL More truth for you.
DAISY Yes.

ROLAND [*realizing it is* MICHEL *onstage*] Where's Michel?

OLIVIER He went to the bathroom.
ROLAND Well that should take all night!
OLIVIER Shhh.

DAISY Is there any truth?
MICHEL Different for each of us. For you it's—
DAISY Yes.
MICHEL You are ugly.
DAISY Yes.
MICHEL You have male genitals.
DAISY [*piteously*] Yes.
MICHEL Get over it.
DAISY How?
MICHEL Many will want to fuck you.
DAISY Who?
MICHEL Perverts.
DAISY And love?
MICHEL A bourgeois sentimental concoction. But—

[*He sits down and takes off his hat. He suddenly looks very much like Foucault. The conversation is suddenly slower and more felt*]

DAISY And love?
MICHEL Yes, you will be loved. If you are honest and proud.
DAISY But all I feel is shame.
MICHEL [*pointing to the closet*] Let him out of the closet, he's obviously gay.

[*He puts on his hat and the farcical tone resumes*]

See you later in the day, after twilight.
DAISY Before dinner.
MICHEL With hors d'oeuvres. Salut. And remember: your own truth is always far easier to face than the general one constructed for you by the dominant culture.
DAISY Thanks.

[MICHEL *exits.* JACQUES *bursts out of his closet*]

JACQUES Well thank Oscar, spending all that time in the closet I finally discovered I'm gay.
BUTLER [*coming out of his closet smoking like Bette Davis*] Curses. Foiled again.

[MICHEL *returns to the audience*]

ROLAND [*to* MICHEL] Did you have a good time in the bathroom?
OLIVIER & DAISY & JACQUES & BUTLER Shhh!

JACQUES [*to* DAISY] Your flower may be fading but your petals are a terse adjective. I feel like a *soupçon* of your smile!
DAISY Let's dance for awhile then. Music, Maestro, please.
DAISY & JACQUES & BUTLER [*singing*]
  We're happy, we're hazy
  We're fundamentally crazy
  We exist in a world all our own
  We're fun, we're stunned
  We're basically on the run
  From all the creatures we know
  Let us entertain you
  And all your morals deride
  We'll kill you, we'll thrill you
  With passions you've always denied
  If you need a reason,
  It's not the season
  for explaining things away
  We're lithe and beguiled
  And happy for awhile
  With the many meanings of gay!
  La la la la ho ho ho
  La la la la ho ho ho
  La la
  Ho ho
  Laaaaaaaaaaaaaaa!

[*Curtain down. Pause. Lights come up in the audience.* MICHEL, ROLAND *and* OLIVIER *applaud with a certain tired, hypnotic somnolence*]

ROLAND Oh my God, I'm tired.
MICHEL Hungry.
ROLAND I had no dinner.
MICHEL Café de Flore.
ROLAND Café de Flore.
OLIVIER Let's!

[*They get up and begin to walk out*]

ROLAND They've refurnished this theatre quite nicely, though on the cheap.
OLIVIER I quite liked the show.
MICHEL The sets were lovely.
ROLAND That's Louis. He's fucking that young director fellow.
MICHEL I didn't know that.
ROLAND It's all very boring.
OLIVIER I thought it was interesting the way the play was able to incorporate the conventions of the well made play while at the same time having a bit of fun with Dumas.

[*Pause.* ROLAND *and* MICHEL *ignore* OLIVIER]

MICHEL I have not been to the Café de Flore for over a month.
ROLAND Oh, my dear, nothing has changed.
MICHEL Absolutely nothing?
ROLAND No. The same Arab lad sits in the corner, drinking from the same Perrier bottle that he fills with tap water, over and over again.

[MICHEL *and* ROLAND *laugh*]

OLIVIER [*trying once more to get* MICHEL'*s attention*] Michel, may I ask you now—just so I can begin thinking about it—is what you are saying in *The History of Sexuality* that we are not actually sexually repressed?

[*He keeps trying to get* MICHEL*'s attention but* MICHEL *is cruising a cute* BOY *who happens to walk by*]

I mean you talk about somehow dispensing with the theory that Western white urban culture had, in a sense, originated sexual repression. You also talk of a kind of risible proliferation of what you call "unorthodox sexualities", and not only this, and I'll try to quote you—to yourself, as it were—you mention some indescribable pattern of operation which is not what we refer to as legal, though you don't deny it is related to the banning of certain desires, that this pattern becomes a kind of link between what you refer to as a glut of "specific pleasures" and "disparate sexualities", in our culture, so, are you saying—

[*They have stopped in front of* ROLAND*'s home*]

ROLAND Oh my, it looks like rain.
MICHEL I don't know. It rained all day.

[*It starts to rain. They all put up their umbrellas*]

ROLAND But [*sighing*] I'm feeling very tired and here we are, in front of my house. I think I shall call it an early evening.
MICHEL But the Café de Flore— I admit, I have missed it this last month—
OLIVIER Well we can still go. Even if Roland is being a wet blanket.
MICHEL Well I suppose we could. [*pause, he looks shyly at* ROLAND] If that is ...
OLIVIER Roland, would you mind?

[*Pause*]

ROLAND [*very stiffly*] Why of course not. Why should I mind? You two have a good time. Don't mind me. I have my Chateaubriand.
MICHEL *Napoleon?*
ROLAND Yes.

MICHEL How marvellous. One just reads and rereads that amazing passage about the exhumation of Napoleon on Sainte-Hélène, because—

ROLAND [*cutting him off*] I agree that is the most pitiful—

[*He looks at the two of them and is discouraged*]

Goodnight.

MICHEL Goodnight Roland.

[*He kisses* ROLAND *in the French way, twice on each cheek*]

OLIVIER Goodnight Roland.

[*Pause.* ROLAND *and* OLIVIER *stare at each other. The absence of a goodnight kiss is acute.* OLIVIER *just waves at* ROLAND]

ROLAND Goodnight.

[MICHEL *and* OLIVIER *walk off, leaving* ROLAND *at his door. Pause*]

ROLAND [*suddenly, impulsively*] Wait!

MICHEL & OLIVIER [*turning*] What?

ROLAND I'm ...

OLIVIER Is something wrong?

ROLAND [*pause*] No ... that is ... I'm going to Morocco.

OLIVIER What?

ROLAND Tomorrow. I've decided I'm going to Morocco, tomorrow.

OLIVIER When did you decide this?

MICHEL What a wonderful idea.

ROLAND I decided weeks ago. I waited to tell you, Olivier. But it's decided I'm going tomorrow.

OLIVIER Oh, well. This is a surprise, I mean—

ROLAND No need to chat about it now. I'll be back of course. And I'll write you both. I just wanted to mention it.

OLIVIER Well, I'll miss you.

ROLAND [*pause*] I'm sure you will. Well, goodnight.

OLIVIER But—

ROLAND But what, Olivier?

OLIVIER But ... have a good time.

ROLAND I plan to. Enjoy the Flore.

[ROLAND *goes towards his house. He stops and eavesdrops*]

OLIVIER What was that all about?

MICHEL I have no idea. Because it was Roland, I assume it was fraught with meaning. To the Flore.

OLIVIER Why yes.

[*They walk*]

But he seemed so melodramatic all of a sudden, you don't suppose, I don't think this could be possible because we stopped having sex ages ago, you don't suppose he's actually jealous?

MICHEL I'd rather not discuss it ...

[*They disappear.* ROLAND *stands, tensely, with his back to his door. He waits for the sound of their footsteps to fade*]

ROLAND Morocco ... I hear ... I hear the climate is mild there ...

[*Lights dim*]

SCENE TWO

Music: the Adagietto from "Les Biches," Poulenc. As the Adagietto
plays the set changes from the dark, dank streets of Paris to the bright
sunlit white expanse of sandy Morocco
Parisian BOYS *set the scene. Suddenly, the* BOYS *run towards the audi-*
ence and roar fiercely. As the music grows calmer they shyly walk back
and look at each other. They slowly remove their Parisian clothing and
become Moroccan BOYS *dressed in European castoffs. The* BOYS *walk*
up to audience members and say, "Would you like to fuck me?". Those
few audience members who say yes are led by the BOYS *to seats on the*
sides of the stage, where they remain seated until the end of Scene
Two
The Adagietto ends. Morocco. Music: "Videntes Stellam," from
Quatre Motets pour le temps de Noël, *Poulenc. One boy,* AMIDOU,
energetically does his exercises. Another boy, YAWEH, *studiously blows a*
piece of fabric in the air. GERARD, *wearing glasses, sits in a corner*
reading a book. He jumps up occasionally and says "Yes! Yes! Yes!" and
then goes back to reading his book, sometimes underlining things.
Three other BOYS *are present. One sells flowers, shyly. Another, rolling*
a baby carriage and approaching audience members saying, "Would
you like to see my baby?" surprises them with the live bunny in the
carriage. Another boy, MUSTAFA, *walks about with a shoe-shining kit,*
yelling "Me, Shine, Chinese"

MUSTAFA You want to know why I need to get money from shining
   shoes? Do you want to know? Well I'll tell you. My grandfather
   you see, my grandfather is a very old man, very old. Dying. So,
   you might ask, and well you might, why I have to get the money?
   Well you see it goes like this in this manner and fashion. My
   grandfather is dying and he wants to write all about what hap-

pened to him in his notebook. His life story. And you might wonder about my grandfather's life. Oh it has been an eventful one. Many wonderful things have happened to him. Saving babies and so forth. And many painful things too. His life has been a veritable cornucopia of eventful happenings. So you see, he must write all this down. It is evident. For future generations. But ahhh, you see, you come to my point, to the climax, in fact, of my discussion: in order to write all this down all these wonderful things— including saving the babies in the middle of a huge storm—he must have a notebook. I mean, how could he write it down otherwise? It is evident to any intelligent person that he needs a notebook. I don't think you need to ask me why. So myself, I am not one who sells pencils or flowers or fruit or animals or other things. I am productive. I am a productive and energetic and hardworking member of society. I do my work. It is to shine. *Me Shine Chinese! Perfect.* I do it perfect for you. *Chinese.* All for my grandfather. Because he needs a notebook and he is dying. And he has led an eventful life. [*he laughs*] To say the least! Saving a baby in the middle of a huge storm, at sea, for instance. This is not charity. This is work for money. Perfect work. *Me Shine Chinese!* For my grandfather. His notebook. To write down his life. Of course, I mean, it is evident.

[ROLAND—*in tourist garb, with camera—wanders among these* BOYS. *It is his first discovery of Morocco. He is in a state of wonder, he is frightened and pleased, he is timid and adventurous—a mass of contradictions. All the* BOYS *drift off, except for* YAWEH, *who is still blowing his piece of fabric in the air. On the last chords of "Videntes Stellam",* YAWEH *tentatively approaches* ROLAND. ROLAND *stares at him*]

YAWEH You see me?

[*Pause*]

You want to touch me?
ROLAND Of course. Of course, I see you. And, of course, I want to touch you. I would like to repeat that memory again.

[YAWEH *walks a few steps back. The final chords of "Videntes Stellam" are replayed.* YAWEH *approaches* ROLAND. *The music ends*]

YAWEH You see me?

[*Pause*]

You want to touch me?
ROLAND Oh my God yes.

[*Tentatively, he moves forward to kiss* YAWEH. *Leaping onto* ROLAND *and pushing him onto his back on the ground,* YAWEH *fucks by rubbing up against him.* YAWEH *comes quickly. Pause. They roll away from each other, still touching, and stare at each other*]

Do you want something from me now?
YAWEH A cigarette?
ROLAND A cigarette? That is all you want?
YAWEH A cigarette.

[ROLAND *lights a cigarette and gives it to* YAWEH *to smoke*]

ROLAND [*to the audience*] All that, for one cigarette. Do you have any idea how many evenings I have spent with Olivier, discussing semiology and art and sex and power and God knows what in order to get one unsatisfying night with him? A night when he would barely touch me, when his orgasm was so torturously long in coming ... and here, this boy is so incredibly passionate and he wants only ... a cigarette. [*to* YAWEH] Are you sure you don't want anything else?
YAWEH [*getting up, as if to go*] Can I come back tomorrow?
ROLAND Of course.

[*Pause*]

I think ... I might be falling in love with you.
YAWEH Tell me where you live.

[ROLAND *whispers to him.* YAWEH *walks off a ways and quietly talks to audience members, ad-lib, about his brother and tomatoes*]

ROLAND And then the next day.

[AMIDOU, *jaunty, mischievous and masculine, walks up to* ROLAND *and taps him on the shoulder*]

AMIDOU Hi.
ROLAND Hello ... what do you want? Why are you here?
AMIDOU It's nature ... [*he grabs his crotch*] It's love!
ROLAND But what do you want?
AMIDOU You suck me off. You give me food. [*he feels himself*] You know, my thing, it's not cut!

[ROLAND *hands him some money*]

ROLAND Here.
AMIDOU I come back tomorrow.
ROLAND Yaweh is coming tomorrow.
AMIDOU In the morning. He's coming in the morning.
ROLAND Well—
AMIDOU I come in the afternoon. You have two in one day, huh? Big man, you can take it!

[*He laughs wildly and runs a ways off.* AMIDOU *quietly talks to audience members, ad-lib, about his uncut penis*]

ROLAND And finally.

[GERARD *enters and taps* ROLAND *on the shoulder*]

GERARD Excuse me, sir.
ROLAND Yes?
GERARD Tonight I have to reflect on Molière's notion of comedy.
ROLAND I see.
GERARD Could you help me?
ROLAND Who sent you?

DAVID HAWE

Christopher Sawchyn as AMIDOU, Jason Cadieux as YAWEH and D. Garnet Harding as GERARD (left to right)

GERARD Amidou.
ROLAND But Amidou is coming over.
GERARD Not until later. You have some time now.
ROLAND But Yaweh—
GERARD Yaweh is sick.

[*Pause*]

So can you tell me what is Molière's notion of comedy?
ROLAND Just a minute, will you?

[GERARD *quietly talks to audience members, ad-lib, about Molière's notion of comedy. All three boys are now saying their speeches at the same time, circling* ROLAND]

YAWEH I'll get you some tomatoes. How many tomatoes do you want? You like my brother? He's younger than me but he has a very big one. If I get the tomatoes then you have to give me some money. For the tomatoes. I could get them now. Or we could fuck now and then I could get the tomatoes. It doesn't matter to me either way.
AMIDOU So you like my thing? It's big enough for you? I thought you would like the long skin. Sometimes guys like to pull on the long skin, I don't mind that. Some boys who aren't cut they don't have as much fun as me. I'm glad I'm not cut. It's too bad you're cut. It's okay though. When I have a son, he won't be cut. He'll have skin like me.
GERARD In reflecting on Molière's notion of comedy we have, of course, the issue of humour. The purpose of humour is to be funny. I think that Molière achieves this purpose through the use of funny situations. People saying funny things. And people doing funny things. Sometimes it is the combined aspect of people saying funny things and people doing funny things that makes Molière's notion of comedy so effective in the theatre.
ROLAND *Boys. Boys. Boys!* Could you just be quiet for a minute!
BOYS Okay.

[*They sit suddenly and are very quiet. They look at each other guiltily*]

ROLAND Now you must understand me. To travel from the dank, dark cold of Paris in the springtime and Olivier who, even if he still somewhere loves me, refuses to fuck me and is probably fucking Michel, even as I stand here in Morocco in the middle of all these boys [*he becomes ecstatic*] and I have three boys, I have three now. Of course there are many more but these three are my favourites.

[*He takes a photograph of the boys. They change their pose as he speaks*]

Each is different in his own way. [*another photograph*] Each has his own quirks, his own special beauty. [*another photograph*] Each is more beautiful than Olivier. [*another photograph*] Each loves me. [*another photograph*]

[*Pause*]

I paused so that you could consider that one. Oh look at the old man giving away pencils and cigarettes and crackers for a fuck. And he calls that love. Don't peruse me like that with your Western eyes. I call it love. And it is love. And if it's not, who cares? I must tell you about them. I must describe them to you in detail, so that you will understand. *Boys!*

[*The* BOYS *jump up*]

BOYS Yes!
ROLAND I have taken the liberty of buying you these nice T-shirts so that everyone can be sure and tell you apart.

[*He pulls three T-shirts from his bag and hands them out*]

You see ... *Y* for Yaweh, *A* for Amidou, and *G* for Gerard.
AMIDOU [*pointing to Gerard's T-shirt*] I like his better!
ROLAND Amidou, you must have *A*, that is the whole point.

[*The three* BOYS *put on their T-shirts and stand there in the T-shirts*]

Now line up ... good ...

[*They line up in such a way that their T-shirts spell out the word "gay".* ROLAND *doesn't like this*]

No, the order is wrong ... Yaweh you go first, Gerard last—
GERARD Why is that, sir, Gerard last? What is the meaning of that?
ROLAND In the order that I met you.
GERARD Oh.

[*They line up so their T-shirts spell out the word "yag". Then* GERARD *decides to fool* ROLAND]

Look, Liza Minelli!

[*He points ahead.* ROLAND *looks. The* BOYS *switch places to spell the word "gay"*]

ROLAND Boys, I told you, order is very important.

[*He makes them spell "yag" again*]

Very good. Now what is important and wonderful about these boys is that they all have stories to tell. And I learn from these stories. Yaweh, your story.

[YAWEH *steps forward*]

YAWEH My mind is empty.
ROLAND Alright. Amidou.

[YAWEH *steps back,* AMIDOU *steps forward*]

AMIDOU I met these three Italians the other day. They all had very short hair and nice silk shirts and ... [*laughing*] this is the joke ... this is the funny joke, they were all very rich but they were of no use to me because—[*laughing hysterically*] because—and this is the funny part ... they thought I was feminine!

213

[GERARD *and* AMIDOU *laugh, uproariously, and then recover*]

YAWEH [*innocently*] You're not?
AMIDOU Hey ... remember this—

[*He grabs* YAWEH]

I'm. [*pause*] Not. [*pause*] Feminine.
YAWEH Okay!

[AMIDOU *lets go of* YAWEH]

AMIDOU Okay.
YAWEH Okay.
AMIDOU *Okay.*
ROLAND [*smiling*] Gerard.

[GERARD *steps forward*]

GERARD A lecture in philosophy.
ROLAND Yes.
GERARD There are four things required of a philosopher.
    1. You must have a certificate in Arabic.
    2. You must travel a great deal.
    3. You must have contacts with other philosophers.
    4. You must be remote from reality.
    Thank you.
ROLAND Excuse me, Gerard.
GERARD Yes sir, how can I help you sir?
ROLAND How would you define "remote from reality"?
GERARD I would define it sir, as for instance, living at the seashore.
ROLAND That would be remote from reality?
GERARD Yes.

[*Pause*]

Or the mountains.
GERARD Or the mountains. Yes.

ROLAND Thank you.

GERARD You're welcome.

[*Pause*]

Or on a cloud.

ROLAND On a cloud?

GERARD A cloud.

ROLAND Yes.

GERARD Yes.

ROLAND Now, the final demonstration for you, so that you will understand the wonder and beauty of these boys and their fundamental differences, I will now demonstrate what each of these boys says when they are at the moment of orgasm. Each is different, and special. Okay, Gerard, you first.

GERARD You said I was last.

ROLAND Last in placement, first for this demonstration.

GERARD Oh.

ROLAND So now demonstrate what you say when you ejaculate.

GERARD Okay.

ROLAND Start by ... masturbating ...

GERARD Okay ... [*he mimes, rather formally*] I'm jacking off now ... oh my oh dear ... oh my goodness ... [*he shouts*] *Watch out, I think I am going to ejaculate! Ahhh.* [*he looks at* ROLAND] How's that?

ROLAND Very precise, Gerard.

GERARD It's best to be precise, to use the right term.

ROLAND Yes. Now Yaweh.

[YAWEH *steps forward*]

Start by masturbating.

YAWEH [*miming masturbation, very intense and concentrated*] I dream ...

ROLAND I dream, Yaweh's word for having an erection—

YAWEH I dream and then ... and then and then ...

ROLAND And then ...

YAWEH And then ... I *burst!* [*he mimes ejaculating*] Ahhhhhh. Whew!

ROLAND Very good.

YAWEH And then I need a cloth to clean up.
ROLAND Yes, Yaweh always likes to have the cloth to clean up.
YAWEH It's messy.

[ROLAND *pats* YAWEH]

ROLAND Very messy yes. I dream, I burst ... and finally, last but not least, [*laughing*] certainly not least, Amidou.
AMIDOU Ready.

[AMIDOU *steps forward*]

ROLAND Masturbate.
AMIDOU I have to use two hands.
ROLAND Yes, Amidou needs two hands.

[AMIDOU *starts to take out his cock*]

Amidou.
AMIDOU What?
ROLAND No. You can't *really* masturbate.
AMIDOU Why not?
ROLAND Because it's illegal.
AMIDOU I don't care.

[GERARD *steps forward*]

GERARD Civilization is when you know your rights and are conscious of your duties!

[AMIDOU *laughs*]

ROLAND What's so funny?
AMIDOU I don't know.
ROLAND Thank you Gerard.
GERARD You're welcome.
ROLAND Civilization tells us we cannot masturbate in public. However you can pretend.
AMIDOU With two hands?

ROLAND Of course, with two hands.

AMIDOU [*beginning to mime masturbation*] Oh God ... oh ... Jesus ... oh ... fuck ... oh ... oh oh oh oh ... [*his is the biggest climax*] Oh my God oh my Jesus lord fuck me Jesus ah ah ah. *Ahhhhhh! Watch out the shit's going to come out now! Arghghghgh!*

[*Pause*]

ROLAND Thank you, Amidou.

AMIDOU You're welcome.

ROLAND [*to audience*] Well I can't tell you how frightening that was the very first time Amidou said, "Watch out, the shit's going to come out now!" Amidou didn't know the word sperm, so he said shit. Very traumatizing.

AMIDOU I still say I'm going to shit.

ROLAND Why Amidou?

AMIDOU I don't know. I like to.

ROLAND So now you have seen my boys perform and demonstrate and you have understood that they love me and I love them.

[*The* BOYS, *remaining in their shirts, go back to their tasks.* GERARD *reads,* YAWEH *blows his fabric in the air and* AMIDOU *exercises*]

Perhaps if you do not understand it is because there are no words in your language; a thing that contains lust and love, that is fleeting and forever, that is contained in the body and yet read with the soul. If I am remote it is because I wish I was a philosopher and as for truth, I prefer parenthesis.

[*Bells jangle*]

Oh, I wonder who that could be? What boy, brother, nephew, beggar, lover?

[YAWEH *places a large wicker chair and cushions on the stage. The stage is now* ROLAND's *room in Morocco.* MICHEL *and* OLIVIER *enter, wearing raincoats and carrying umbrellas: very Parisian.* MICHEL *also wears a leather jacket and boots and a leather military cap.* OLIVIER *looks like a schoolboy. They both carry baggage]*

Olivier, Michel, what a surprise!

[OLIVIER *runs up to* ROLAND *and kisses him*]

OLIVIER We're sorry, Roland. We wrote you and you didn't write back, we hoped you wouldn't mind. We can stay in a hotel if it's inconvenient.
ROLAND Why no, not at all, are you travelling together?
OLIVIER [*uncomfortable*] Well, ahhh, yes.

[*Pause*]

ROLAND Why then there is a double mat in the guest room. I will reserve it for you. Michel. How are you?
MICHEL [*putting down his bag*] Dying.
ROLAND [*staring at him*] Michel, I—
MICHEL Don't pity me. It is *only* the body, as they say, which is interesting to watch even when it disintegrates. How can it be a source of power when it is not a source of weakness also?

[GERARD *gets up from reading and enters the group*]

GERARD Excuse me, sir.
ROLAND Yes Gerard.
GERARD Must a play have a plot?
ROLAND Not always.
GERARD Must it have characters?
ROLAND Not always.
GERARD Must it have poetry?
ROLAND It is advisable, if the play has neither plot nor characters, that it have poetry.
GERARD Good. I stayed up late last night, as poets do, writing verses. Do you wish to hear them? [*he begins*] Ahem. "I have a bird, I've named her twitty. If I sit in sand, my bum gets gritty."
ROLAND [*smiling*] Thank you, Gerard.
GERARD I'll read you more later. After we fuck.

DAVID HAWE

Mark Lonergan as **OLIVIER** and Randall Lanthier as **ROLAND** (left to right)

[GERARD *walks by* OLIVIER, *suddenly noticing him. He looks* OLIVIER *over and speaks to* MICHEL]

You can find a much better boy than that, here.

[*He walks away*]

OLIVIER [*miffed*] Who was that?
ROLAND Gerard. He's a friend. He can sometimes be brutally frank.
OLIVIER Michel, I am going to lie down.

[*He walks over and kisses* MICHEL *on the cheek, eyeing* ROLAND]

The bedroom?
ROLAND The mat is in there.

[OLIVIER *goes off, glancing at* MICHEL. *Pause*]

MICHEL Is there somewhere for me to sit down?
ROLAND A cushion, on the floor.

[*He throws* MICHEL *a cushion*]

A drink, some kif?

[*He sits in the wicker chair*]

MICHEL A drink, thank you.
ROLAND Yaweh.
YAWEH Yes?
ROLAND Two cognacs please.
YAWEH Yes.

[*He goes off*]

MICHEL I am amazed.
ROLAND You needn't be.
MICHEL I should not be amazed that someone who has removed himself

from the theatre of political activism should so easily be subsumed by the maxims of colonialism.

ROLAND You are angry because I treated him like a servant.

[YAWEH *enters, balancing the drinks carefully*]

MICHEL I am annoyed because it is necessary for you to become a servant to the predominant modes of power. If, perhaps, you had attempted to understand the psychological intricacies of sado-masochism then you would not need to oppress these poor children.

ROLAND Did you come thousands of miles to insult me?

[MICHEL *smiles, taking a cognac from* YAWEH]

MICHEL Hundreds.

ROLAND I won't be berated because I am uninterested in having a whip taken to my buttocks. Surely you of all people should understand desire. Sadomasochism is not mine.

MICHEL I am not disparaging you. I am merely speaking in the context of the multiplicity of sexualities.

ROLAND [*tired*] Ahhh, the lecture.

[*He takes the second cognac.* YAWEH *leaves*]

MICHEL No, listen. Therein lies the difference, in that grey zone that we call consensual. [*savouring the word*] Consensual ... con-sensual. When I whip somebody I have their permission. Your emotional domination of these children is without their consent. It's all a question of class, really. You're a closet classist—

ROLAND [*interrupting, a slight quaver in his voice*] Is Olivier your lover now?

MICHEL Olivier.

[*Pause. He lowers his voice*]

I don't mind telling you he desperately wants to be. I have never met such a confirmed bottom in my entire life. He would lick my

Mark Christmann as **MICHEL** (front) and Randall Lanthier as **ROLAND** (rear)

DAVID HAWE

boots, if I would have him. [*sighing*] Yes, he is in love with me.
Yes, he has moved in with me. Yes, he would be with me twenty-
four hours of the day. Yes, he would kiss me constantly, every time
he leaves the room. No, I won't have him in my bed. You know
the hard bodies I prefer. And the hard of mind. But he is convenient to have around. Of course when he started writing me
poems, I ...

[ROLAND *stands up, his hand is shaking*]

ROLAND Stop.
MICHEL Pardon me.
ROLAND *Stop!*
MICHEL Oh, I'm sorry.

[*Pause*]

Have I upset you?
ROLAND [*carefully*] I know that you are ill, and—[*to himself*] for once
in your life, get angry—[*to* MICHEL] How do you think I feel? I
have been in love with him!
MICHEL With who—
ROLAND *With Olivier you idiot! How do you think it feels to know that
he will do everything for you and nothing for me! Have you no idea
how it drives a knife through my heart to hear those things? Have you
no idea—*

[*As* ROLAND *rages* GERARD, AMIDOU *and* YAWEH *come out of the
other parts of the house and watch the argument, silently, in wonder*]

MICHEL [*flabbergasted*] Honestly I—
ROLAND The damage is done. Perhaps now you know. I feel things. I
do not always express it, but it is true.
MICHEL I'm sorry— [*he goes towards* ROLAND]
ROLAND Don't touch me.

[*Pause.* OLIVIER *enters*]

OLIVIER Is something wrong?

ROLAND *Why did you have to come here!*

[*He runs to* OLIVIER, *starts to embrace him madly and then hits him*]

Why why why!

OLIVIER I'm sorry Roland. I *honestly* didn't know.

[MICHEL *wrenches them apart*]

MICHEL Olivier, go back to bed.

OLIVIER Sorry.

[ROLAND *is crying.* OLIVIER *leaves.* GERARD *and* YAWEH *wander off. Lights dim. It is dusk.* AMIDOU *wanders over to* ROLAND]

AMIDOU Roland?

ROLAND What?

AMIDOU Can I have an aspirin?

ROLAND Why do you want an aspirin?

AMIDOU You gave one to Yaweh.

ROLAND Yaweh had a headache.

AMIDOU If I have a headache will you give me an aspirin?

ROLAND Yes.

AMIDOU I have a headache.

ROLAND In the bathroom, in the red bottle.

AMIDOU Thank you.

[*He looks at* ROLAND *and* MICHEL *strangely and exits*]

MICHEL They are charming.

[*Pause*]

ROLAND Of course they are charming. They speak another language.

[*Pause*]

MICHEL If only you had come out.

ROLAND Oh dear, I hate this homosexual lingo. What good would that do?

MICHEL Pride. Clarity.

ROLAND I am quite happy in my shame and my confusion. You, Michel, will never understand the importance of the parenthesis.

MICHEL [*kidding him*] Ahhh, the lecture.

ROLAND [*almost smiling*] Now, now—and this "coming out" is just a recent thing with you, surely. You used to think it was unnecessary.

MICHEL For political reasons. But when I went to Toronto and saw the power of the asses swaying, in the gay parade—

[*Pause*]

ROLAND And what about this disease?

MICHEL What about it?

ROLAND I don't mean to be callous and treat you like a "case", but it seems to me … [*he sniffles*] that this horrible disease is going to make your gay liberation a thing of the past.

MICHEL No, it will not.

ROLAND How can you say that? It is very evident to me that the dominant culture has consistently viewed homosexuality as a metaphor for sickness and death. This disease is becoming associated with gay men. What hope do we have now?

[*Music: the finale of "Dialogues des Carmelites," Poulenc*]

MICHEL Listen. Listen …

ROLAND What?

MICHEL Shhh. Listen.

[*The murmur of the crowd from the "Dialogues des Carmelites" is heard. Lights dim. The* BOYS *begin marching slowly up a ladder to the scaffold as* MICHEL *speaks. They walk along a precipice and with the noise of the slice of the knife—from "Dialogues"—they fall one by one and disappear. They then continue up the scaffold again. This is repeated over and over*]

Hear that? I have a vision of this disease. And my vision is this. Many will die. It will be called a plague. Mankind will be called upon to test itself. Mankind will fail the test. In America they will assume that all the undesirables, all the black people, all the sexual people, all the whores will die and the dominant culture will triumph. But listen.

[*The women from "Dialogues des Carmelites" begin singing*]

But no, for every faggot that dies, ten are born, and those ten more are born with a clearer vision of who they are. Why they are here. The power they have here, between their legs. Between their thighs. In their eyes. Listen, can you not hear? Can you not see them?

ROLAND Now it is you who is being sentimental—

MICHEL If only I was. I am not. If you want to see the angels, you must look up ...

[*"Dialogues des Carmelites" swells.* MICHEL *begins shouting over the music*]

Look up, see the angels! They will not disappear! They will not be vanquished. We are the only ones who are willing to tell the truth. Look up! Look at them! Are they turning back? Or are they not just becoming more confirmed more dogmatic more inflexible more passionate more obscene more divine. Do you hear me? More divine. Look at them! Look up! They are more divine!

[*The music stops*]

ROLAND More divine. I'm looking up. I see nothing.

[*The music begins again and plays very softly. The boys continue to march and to fall*]

MICHEL It doesn't matter. It really doesn't matter if anyone sees it, if anyone realizes for a very long time. For it will be.

ROLAND It is a natural impulse to romanticize one's own death.

226

Michel, you must know that however you have hurt me and however you will continue to hurt me, I love you. You are an influen-
tial man, perhaps a great man. There is no need for you to build a
myth out of this disease.

MICHEL I'm not. It is one, it will be one. Look up?

ROLAND Are they still there?

MICHEL Why yes, Roland, even your boys. Even your boys will be on
the scaffold. Your little slaves that you will not admit are your
slaves, they will be there too, yes.

ROLAND We are getting very morbid in our old age.

MICHEL And I am not even old. [*he starts to cry*]

[ROLAND *holds* MICHEL. *Pause.* OLIVIER *enters, the music stops again
at the sound of the first cut of the knife*]

OLIVIER I can't sleep on a grass mat.

ROLAND I had a feeling you would find it uncomfortable, Olivier.

MICHEL Perhaps we shouldn't have come.

OLIVIER Can we go home, Michel? You two are fighting and—you are ill.

MICHEL Perhaps it's best. [*to* ROLAND] Where's the bathroom?

ROLAND That way.

MICHEL Excuse me.

[*Uncomfortable pause*]

ROLAND I don't think Michel will like the bathroom.

OLIVIER Why? Because it's outside?

ROLAND No. Unlike Paris, here no one cruises the bathrooms. The sex
is too available on the street.

[*Pause*]

OLIVIER I missed you, Roland.

ROLAND I didn't miss you at all.

[*Pause*]

Until now.

[*Pause*]

Now I miss you very much.

OLIVIER You seem very happy here with your rude little boys.

ROLAND I'm never happy.

[*Pause*]

If you go back to Paris, I will follow you.

OLIVIER But, Roland—

ROLAND I know you are not in love with me. I know you are in love
with Michel. But for some reason I am in love with you. I don't
think I am "in love" with these boys. Love—what a stupid bourgeois notion—learned from television ads. Yes, I think I am in
love with you. Perhaps because there is no reason to be in love
with you. Perhaps just because your body is soft and your nails are
dirty.

[OLIVIER *examines his nails*]

And you have tried so desperately to enjoy Proust. Perhaps because
you treat me badly. Perhaps these boys don't treat me badly
enough. I will follow you. And you will be in love with Michel,
and Michel will be in love with no one. Because, that is, I imagine, the way it always will be. End of speech.

OLIVIER Roland I … I enjoy your company.

ROLAND I have nothing more to say. As Yaweh says, I am empty.

[MICHEL *returns*]

MICHEL No glory holes.

ROLAND No.

MICHEL We're off, as quickly as we came.

OLIVIER We didn't even unpack.

ROLAND See you in Paris.

[MICHEL *and* ROLAND *hug*]

Goodbye my friend.

MICHEL See you soon.

[*They walk off,* OLIVIER *whispering to* MICHEL *animatedly. Pause.* AMIDOU *appears suddenly*]

AMIDOU That was good aspirin.

ROLAND How many did you take?

AMIDOU Four.

ROLAND Well I suppose it won't do you any harm. You might get a stomach ache.

AMIDOU Yaweh didn't.

[*Pause*]

You want to fuck?

ROLAND Yes, Amidou, I want to fuck. But first …

[*He picks up his camera.* GERARD, AMIDOU *and* YAWEH *gather for the photos and take several poses. Music: the last notes of "Videntes Stellam," followed by the final-minute of "Aubade," both Poulenc. The audience members on the stage are asked by Parisian* BOYS *to return to their seats. Lights dim*]

SCENE THREE

Paris. Rain. Only one dark room appears: ROLAND'*s home.* ROLAND *is sitting in the*
chair reading his oversized Chateaubriand when a bedraggled but surly
Parisian street-boy, HOOKER, *wearing a beret, knocks at his door*

ROLAND Yes?

HOOKER Excuse me sir?

ROLAND Yes?

HOOKER You gave me your address.

ROLAND I did?

HOOKER Last week, at the Cafe de Florry or something?

ROLAND Ahhh yes, I seem to remember—

HOOKER You told me I reminded you of someone. I don't know.

ROLAND Ahhh, yes, won't you come in.

[*Pause*]

You're wet.

HOOKER Yeah. It's raining.

ROLAND Perhaps you should get out of those wet things.

HOOKER Sure.

[*The* HOOKER *strips naked except for the beret which hides his face.*
He stands shivering in the damp room]

ROLAND Take off your hat.

HOOKER But I like my hat.

ROLAND If you wish. Here.

[*He hands him a blanket*]

HOOKER Thank you.
ROLAND You do look familiar.

[*Pause*]

Have you ever been to Morocco?
HOOKER [*lying*] No.

[*Pause*]

I don't have it.
ROLAND What?
HOOKER The disease.
ROLAND That's not what I meant.

[*Pause*]

HOOKER I'll suck your cock for fifty francs. But for a hundred and fifty francs you can fuck me.

[*Pause*]

ROLAND I don't have any condoms.
HOOKER It doesn't matter. [*pause*] I have to eat.

[*Pause.* ROLAND *sits back down in the chair*]

ROLAND Take off that blanket.
HOOKER It's cold.
ROLAND I know.

[*Pause. He drops the blanket*]

Turn around.

[*He does*]

ROLAND Thank you. Here.

[*He gives him one hundred and fifty francs*]

HOOKER Thank you sir.

[*He suddenly gets bouncy and—for a moment—takes on* GERARD's *accent*]

Now I can reflect on Molière's notion of comedy!
ROLAND What was that?
HOOKER [*returning to normal*] Nothing, sir.
ROLAND You seem so happy.
HOOKER I have a hundred and fifty francs. I'm going to get drunk.
ROLAND I thought you said you were going to eat.
HOOKER I'm going to get drunk first. I won't need much because I haven't eaten for two days. I'll eat tomorrow.
ROLAND Here, let me buy you dinner—
HOOKER No, I'm going to Le Palace.
ROLAND Le Palace?
HOOKER Yes.
ROLAND Where is that?
HOOKER Right around the corner. You want to come?
ROLAND Oh, I never go to those places, I'm getting too old.
HOOKER No you're not. There's lots of old guys like you there. It's great. It used to be an old theatre. They redid it.
ROLAND Well, I don't know.
HOOKER Come on. It'll be fun—
ROLAND But it's a disco—
HOOKER It's a place for everybody. You *have* to come. [*he gets campy*] Marcel says it's just *more divine* than anything!
ROLAND More divine?
HOOKER [*impatient*] Come on!
ROLAND Just a minute.

[*Pause.* ROLAND *stands and turns to the audience*]

There shall be time, I expect, for crying, if it is absolutely necessary.

HOOKER [*jubilant*] Come on—you can buy me dinner!

ROLAND Why not? [*to the audience*] Come with us. Come along.

[ROLAND *and the* HOOKER *go out the door. Music: the climax of "Le Repas de Midi," Poulenc. Red drapery begins to fall and grand chandeliers descend. Fags, dykes, boys, chicks, women, men, whores, old, young—all kinds—appear. Drag queens and marvellously beautiful muscle boys, with grand animal heads, march down a grand staircase. Leather couples gather in the corners and flirt and play. Everyone laughs and begins to dance. The Poulenc ends and disco begins and everyone begins to party.* ROLAND *seems to be enjoying himself, dancing with* GERARD. MICHEL *and* OLIVIER *are finally necking in some corner*]

[*End*]

SKY GILBERT

Playwright, poet, actor and drag queen extraordinaire … Sky Gilbert is one of Canada's most controversial artistic forces. As the co-founder and Artistic Director of Buddies in Bad Times Theatre—Canada's largest gay and lesbian theatre—Gilbert has written and directed his own hit plays, including *The Dressing Gown* (published by Playwrights Union, 1989), *Drag Queens on Trial*, *The Postman Rings Once*, *Ban This Show* (about Robert Mapplethorpe), *Capote at Yaddo* (published by Coach House Press, 1992), and *Play Murder* (published by Blizzard, July 1995). Through Buddies' *RHUBARB!* and *QUEERCULTURE* Festivals, Gilbert helps to nurture and inspire other young artists and to ensure a strong and alternative cultural voice in Canada. His credits as a director of others' work are extensive. For the Shaw Festival, Gilbert directed Oscar Wilde's *Anything Goes*, *Salomé* and was the assistant director for the original Shaw Festival production of Edmond Rostand's *Cyrano de Bergerac*. Other critically acclaimed productions directed by Gilbert include: *Treatment*, by Jonathan Moore, for Another Stage and *How I Wonder What You Are*, by Robert Morgan, for Theatre Direct. Gilbert received the Pauline McGibbon Award for directing in 1985; a Dora Mavor Moore Award for Best New Play, Small Theatres Category, for his script *The Whore's Revenge* in 1990; a Dora Mavor Moore Award for Best Production, Small Theatres Category, in 1992, for his direction of his own comedy *Suzie Goo: Private Secretary*; and in 1994 he was nominated for a Chalmers Award for *Play Murder*. His plays have been produced in New York, Chicago, San Francisco, Houston, Vancouver, Montreal, Phoenix and Seattle as well as Toronto. He has produced three movies, including *My Addiction*, presented at Cinq Jours Du Cinema Independent Canadien in Montreal in 1994. His newest play, *Jim Dandy*, premiered at Buddies in Fall 1995.